finboroughtheatre

The world premiere of

The Six-Days World

by Elizabeth Kuti

First performance at the Finborough Theatre, London
Wednesday 28 November 2007

The author gratefully acknowledges the support of the Arts and Humanities Research Council. With thanks also to the National Theatre Studio, especially Chris Campbell, Sebastian Born, Purni Morrell, Jack Bradley and Lucy Davis.

Arts & Humanities
Research Council

The Six-Days World

by Elizabeth Kuti

Cast in order of appearance
Ralph **William Whymper**
Angela **Katharine Barker**
Eddie **Chris Moran**
Cat **Tracy Kearney**
Kirsty **Rosalind Porter**
Tom **Robert Emms**

Director **Jamie Harper**
Designer **James Lewis**
Lighting **Adam Bullock**
Sound **Tomas Gisby** and **Neil Townsend**
Costume Designer **Nicky Bunch**
Nativity Carvings **Eliza Kentridge**
           with thanks to Guy Taplin and John Fletcher

The play is set in a small town in the South East of England on
Christmas Eve, 2007.

The performance lasts approximately two hours.

There will be one interval of fifteen minutes.

The Six-Days World was given a rehearsed reading at the National Theatre
Studio on 31 July 2007, directed by Jamie Harper, with cast as follows:

Angela **Susan Brown**
Ralph **Michael Cronin**
Eddie **Ross Waiton**
Kirsty **Charlotte Pyke**
Tom **James Powell**
Cat **Polly Lister**

Katharine Barker Angela

Katharine trained at the Central School of Speech and Drama. Theatre includes *Henry V*, *The Merchant of Venice*, and *The Jew of Malta* (Royal Shakespeare Company); *Indian Ink*, *The Winter's Tale*, *Macbeth*, *Rutherford and Son*, *The Taming of the Shrew*, *Waters of the Moon* and *To Kill a Mockingbird* (all at Salisbury Playhouse); *Hay Fever* (Oxford Stage Company); *To Kill a Mockingbird*, *Ion*, *Macbeth*, *Three Sisters*, *The Europeans*, *Blood Wedding* and *The Crucible* (Mercury, Colchester); *Anna Karenina* (three UK and international tours for Shared Experience); *Out of the Crocodile* (Phoenix); *Ballad of the False Barman* (Hampstead Theatre); *Twelfth Night* (Old Bankside Globe); *The Snow Queen* (Young Vic); *What About Leonardo?* (Lilian Baylis); *The Witches* (Vaudeville) and most recently a workshop production of Peter Handke's *The Hour We Knew Nothing of Each Other* (National Theatre Studio). TV includes *The Ha-Ha*, *The Wedding Night*, *Breaking it Gently*, *Dear Janet Rosenberg Dear Mr Kooning* (Granada); *Emmerdale Farm* (Yorkshire); *Widows* (Euston Films); *The System* (HTV) and *My Little Eye* (Channel 4). Film includes *Morris Loves Birds* and *The Ultimate Cocktail*. Radio includes *Exchanges in Bialystok*.

Robert Emms Tom

Robert trained at LAMDA, graduating earlier this year. Theatre includes rehearsed readings of *Hebron* (National Theatre); *The Knave in the Grain* (Shakespeare's Globe); *Equus* (Edinburgh Festival); *Antony and Cleopatra* (Sam Wanamaker Festival at Shakespeare's Globe); *Shopping and F***ing* and *Anna Karenina* (LAMDA). TV includes *Waking the Dead* (BBC). Film includes *Bucco Blanco* (Zoom Films Global).

Tracy Kearney Cat

At the Finborough Theatre, Tracy appeared in *The Ladies' Cage*, and the subsequent transfer to the Manchester Royal Exchange. Other theatre includes *The Donor* (King's Head); *Closer* (Gateway); *A Midsummer Night's Dream* (St George's, Tufnell Park); *Human Anatomies* (Hen and Chickens); *Can't Stand Up for Falling Down* (Granary, Ireland); *A Wilde Night* (The Firkin Crane, Ireland); and *Sexual Perversity in Chicago* (Cork Arts). Film and TV includes *The Magdalene Sisters* (winner of the Golden Lion at the Venice Film Festival); *Talking with Angels* (BAFTA nominated, and shortlisted for an Academy Award); *The Welcome Committee* (British Council); *The Green Green Grass* and *Doctors* (BBC). Radio includes *The Death of Faith* (BBC Radio 4).

Chris Moran Eddie

Chris graduated from LAMDA in 2003 and won the Carleton Hobbs Bursary Award, leading to six months as a member of the BBC Radio Drama Company. Theatre includes *Dead Hands* (Riverside Studios) and *Animaux en Paradis* (Theatre Deux Rives, Rouen), both with Howard Barker's company The Wrestling School; *My Boy Jack* (national tour); *Donkey's Years* (West End); *Making History* (Irish tour) and *Treading the Boards* (Rosemary Branch). Radio for the BBC includes *Volpone*, *Richard II*, *The Pallisers*, *Hard Times*, *Venus and Adonis* and Howard Barker's *The Moving and the Still*.

Rosalind Porter Kirsty

Rosalind trained at LAMDA. Theatre includes *Peapickers* (Eastern Angles Theatre Company); *There* (Royal Court); *Petrograd* (Pleasance, Edinburgh); *Feeding Time* (BAC). TV includes *Family Affairs* (Channel Five Productions). Film includes *Shadowboxing* (BBC).

William Whymper Ralph

William trained at the Guildford School of Acting. Theatre includes *Julius Caesar*, *Richard III*, *Henry IV* (*Parts I* and *II*); *Much Ado About Nothing*, *Antony and Cleopatra* (Royal Shakespeare Company); *Butley*, *The Cherry Orchard* (Farnham); *Deathtrap*, *Educating Rita* (Colchester); *When We Are Married* (Ipswich); *A Flea in Her Ear*, *Saved*, *The Norman Conquests*, *Twelfth Night* (Leeds); *Saint Joan* (Oldham); *Hamlet* (Royal Shakespeare

Company Fringe); *The Caretaker* (Woking); *Quartet* (Perth); *Sleuth* (Geneva); *The Father* (Theatre Royal, Stratford East); *Jackets II* (Bush); *The Revenger's Tragedy* (Southwark Playhouse). TV includes *The Mayor of Casterbridge, Richard II, Henry V, King John, The Borgias, Crown Court, By the Sword Divided, Juliet Bravo, Animal Behaviour, Strangers and Brothers, The Collectors, Just William, Hetty Wainthropp Investigates* and *Bomber*.

Elizabeth Kuti Playwright

Elizabeth Kuti's most recent play was *The Sugar Wife* (Rough Magic Theatre Company at Soho and Project Arts Centre, Dublin), which was joint winner of the Susan Smith Blackburn Award, and nominated for Best New Play in The Irish Times Theatre Awards. Other plays include *The Whisperers*, a completion of Frances Sheridan's 18th-century comedy *A Trip to Bath* (Rough Magic Theatre Company on Irish tour and at the Traverse, Edinburgh); *Treehouses* (National Theatre of Ireland, Peacock at the Abbey, Dublin, Northcott, Exeter), which won second prize in the Susan Smith Blackburn Awards and the BBC Radio Drama Prize in the Stewart Parker Awards; and *The Countrywoman* (Upstate Theatre Project at the Civic Theatre, Dublin, and Drogheda Arts Centre). She has also written two short plays for the Miniaturists – *Time Spent on Trains* (Southwark Playhouse), and *Eighty Miles* (Arcola). Radio plays include two Afternoon Plays for BBC Radio 4 – *May Child* starring Patricia Routledge, and *The Glasswright*; and *Mr Fielding's Scandal-Shop*, broadcast on BBC Radio 3 on Christmas Day 2005. She is also currently writing a new play commissioned by the Abbey Theatre, Dublin.

Jamie Harper Director

Jamie studied English Literature at the University of Sheffield. After graduating, he spent two years in America directing at various theatres including the Actors' Studio in New York and the Boston Directors' Lab. He returned to the UK to train on the directors' course at LAMDA and he has regularly taught and directed at the Academy over the last three years. Recent directing work includes *The Things Good Men Do* (Old Red Lion and Lyric Hammersmith Studio); *The Vanek Plays* (Operating Theatre Company and Tristan Bates); *The Infant* (Old Red Lion and Gilded Balloon); *A Lie of the Mind* (BAC); and an improvised play for the BBC Radio Drama programme, 'From Fact to Fiction'. Assistant directing credits include *Oedipus The King* (National Theatre Studio); *Mother Courage and Her Children* (English Touring Theatre); *Merry Christmas Betty Ford* (Lyric, Belfast) and *Love and a Bottle* (Young Vic). He will also be working as Staff Director on James Macdonald's forthcoming production of *The Hour We Knew Nothing of Each Other* (National Theatre). He is the winner of the 2006 JMK Directors' Award and the 2006 John S. Cohen Bursary for which he was Resident Director at English Touring Theatre and the National Theatre Studio.

James Lewis Designer

James studied Theatre Design and Production at The University of Wales in Carmarthen, graduating in 2003. Recent design credits include *Minor Spectacular* (national tour); *These Four Walls* (Debut Theatre Company at Newbury Corn Exchange); *Kiss of Life* (Sydney Opera House); *Rebus McTaggart: Crime Warrior* (national tour); *Space 50* (ICA); and *Hot Pursuit* (UK and New Zealand tours). James has also built sets for the West End, national and international tours, and has travelled the world with several theatre companies as a Technical Manager.

Tomas Gisby and Neil Townsend Sound

Tomas Gisby and Neil Townsend formed Ex Animo Productions in 1999 to create original sound and music for a variety of different media including film, multimedia, theatre and other live performance. Recent designs for theatre include *The Germinator* (Assembly Rooms, Edinburgh) and *Les Enfants Terribles* for which they also composed and performed an original score. Sound work for television includes *FM* (Room 5 Productions for Channel 4).

Nicky Bunch Costume Designer

Nicky trained at the Central School of Speech and Drama. For the Finborough Theatre, she designed the set for *The Lower Depths* and set and costumes for *Loyalties* and *IWitness*. Other set and costume design credits include *Wuthering Heights, Twelfth Night* (National Tour and Riverside Studios for the Love and Madness Ensemble); *Love Me Dorothy* and *Pretty Please* (Greenwich Playhouse); *Strangers* (Oval House Theatre); *Uncle Vanya* (Tristan Bates); *Endgame* (Pentameters); *The Playboy of the Western World* (national tour); *Breasts and Burgers* (Edinburgh Festival); *The Balcony* (Embassy); and costume supervision for two site specific productions of *Underground* (dreamthinkspeak). Forthcoming projects include *The Winter's Tale* (Courtyard Theatre) and *Jesus Christ Superstar* (Arts Educational Schools).

finboroughtheatre

www.finboroughtheatre.co.uk
Artistic Director **Neil McPherson**
Associate Directors **John Terry, Kate Wasserberg**
Resident Designer **Alex Marker**
Associate Designer **Nicky Bunch**
Pearson Playwright-in-Residence **Al Smith**
Playwrights-in-Residence
         James Graham, Peter Oswald, Laura Wade, Alexandra Wood
Literary Manager **Jane Fallowfield**
General Manager **Cara Dunkling**
Resident Assistant Director **Alexander Summers**
Development Producer **Rachel Payant**
The Finborough Theatre has the support of the Pearson Playwrights' Scheme, supported by the Peggy Ramsay Foundation

finboroughtheatre

Founded in 1980, the multi-award-winning Finborough Theatre under Artistic Director Neil McPherson presents new writing from the UK and overseas, music theatre and unjustly neglected work from the last 150 years.

In its first decade, artists working at the theatre included Rory Bremner, Clive Barker, Kathy Burke, Nica Burns, Ken Campbell and Clare Dowie. In the early 1990s, the theatre was at the forefront of new writing with Naomi Wallace's first play *The War Boys*; Rachel Weisz in David Farr's *Neville Southall's Washbag* which later became the award-winning West End play, *Elton John's Glasses*; and three plays by Anthony Neilson – *The Year of the Family*, *Normal* and *Penetrator*, which went on to play at the Royal Court. From 1994, the theatre was run by The Steam Industry. Highlights included new plays by Tony Marchant, David Eldridge, Mark Ravenhill and Phil Willmott, new writing development including Mark Ravenhill's *Shopping and F***king* (Royal Court, West End and Broadway) and Naomi Wallace's *Slaughter City* (Royal Shakespeare Company); the UK premiere of David Mamet's *The Woods*, and Anthony Neilson's *The Censor*, which transferred to the Royal Court.

Neil McPherson became Artistic Director in 1999. New British plays since then have included the world premieres of Sarah Phelps' *Modern Dance for Beginners* (subsequently produced at the Soho Theatre); Carolyn Scott-Jeffs' *Out in the Garden* (which transferred to the Assembly Rooms, Edinburgh); a number of plays specially commissioned for the Finborough including Laura Wade's London debut with her adaptation of W.H. Davies' *Young Emma*, and James Graham's *Eden's Empire and Little Madam*; Simon Vinnicombe's *Year 10* which went on to play at BAC's Time Out Critics' Choice Season; James Graham's *Albert's Boy* with Victor Spinetti; and Joy Wilkinson's *Fair* which transferred to the West End. London premieres include Paulo Coelho's *The Alchemist*, Sonja Linden's *I Have Before Me a Remarkable Document Given to Me by a Young Lady from Rwanda*; and Jack Thorne's *Fanny and Faggot* (which has just transferred to the West End).

UK premieres of foreign plays have included Brad Fraser's *Wolfboy*; Lanford Wilson's *Sympathetic Magic*; Larry Kramer's *The Destiny of Me*; Tennessee Williams' *Something Cloudy, Something Clear*; Frank McGuinness' *Gates of Gold* with William Gaunt and the late John Bennett in his last stage role (which also transferred to the West End); *Hortensia and the Museum of Dreams* with Linda Bassett; *Blackwater Angel*, the UK debut of Irish playwright Jim Nolan with Sean Campion; and Joshua Sobol's *iWitness*.

Revivals of neglected work have included the first London revivals of Rolf Hochhuth's *Soldiers*, and *The Representative*; both parts of Keith Dewhurst's *Lark Rise to Candleford*, performed in promenade and in repertoire; *The Gigli Concert* with Niall Buggy, Catherine Cusack and Paul McGann (which transferred to the Assembly Rooms, Edinburgh); *The Women's War*, an evening of original suffragette plays; the Victorian comedy *Masks and Faces*; *Etta Jenks* with Clarke Peters and Daniela Nardini; *Loyalties* by John Galsworthy; Noël Coward's first play, *The Rat Trap*; T.W. Robertson's *Ours*; Robert McLellan's *Jamie the Saxt*, written in Scots; and the acclaimed Celebrating British Music Theatre series reviving forgotten British musicals, particularly from 1880-1920.

The Finborough Theatre has for three years running has been the only unfunded theatre to win the prestigious Pearson Award bursary for writers Chris Lee in 2000, Laura Wade in 2005, James Graham in 2006 and Al Smith in 2007 – as well as the Pearson Award for Best Play for Laura Wade in 2005. The Finborough Theatre was the inaugural winner of the Empty Space Peter Brook Award's Dan Crawford Pub Theatre Award in 2005, won the Empty Space Peter Brook Mark Marvin Award in 2004 and was shortlisted in 2006 and 2007, and was shortlisted for the Empty Space Peter Brook Award for Up-and-Coming Venues in 2003, and for Studio Theatres in 2007.

You can find out more about the theatre and its work – and buy Finborough play texts – at **www.finboroughtheatre.co.uk**

Engine against th' Almightie, sinners towre,
Reversed thunder, Christ-side-piercing spear,
The six-daies world transposing in an houre

George Herbert, 'Prayer'

THE SIX-DAYS WORLD

for the Price boys
Charlie and Robin and Robert

Characters

RALPH, *sixty-eight*
ANGELA, *seventy-one, Ralph's wife*
EDDIE, *thirty-five, their son*
KIRSTY, *thirty-three, landlady of The Greyhound*
TOM, *nineteen*
CAT, *thirty-six, lives with Eddie*

Scene One: Garage
Scene Two: Sitting room
Scene Three: Pub
Scene Four: Sitting room
Scene Five: Garage

The play is set in a small town in the south east of England. Christmas Eve, 2007.

A forward slash in the text (/) indicates the point of interruption by the next speaker.

This text went to press before the end of rehearsals and so may differ slightly from the play as performed.

Scene One

December 24th.

The garage of a modest suburban semi-detached house.

It has not been used for cars but has been adapted into a workshop for carpentry.

There are three tea chests in the middle of the floor. The lids are nailed shut.

About 4.30 pm.

Cold blue-ish light.

RALPH *is there, looking at the chests.*

Enter ANGELA, *holding a coat.*

ANGELA. Why not just leave them?

RALPH. I want to look.

ANGELA. You're only making more work. They could go straight into the boot as they are.

RALPH. I want to make sure nothing's missing.

ANGELA. Have you got one of those – whatja-ma – for getting the nails up –

RALPH. Yes.

ANGELA. I think there's one in the –

RALPH. I know where there's one.

He exits.

ANGELA. I brought you your coat.

ANGELA *approaches the tea chests.*

She reaches out to touch one but before she does, RALPH *returns with an implement for prising open tea chests.*

I don't know if I've made a mistake with that icing.

RALPH. What sort of mistake?

ANGELA. I used that natural-coloured sugar but that means it's come out off-white.

RALPH. Brown.

ANGELA. Yes.

RALPH. You did that last year.

ANGELA. Did I?

RALPH. Yes.

ANGELA. I must have forgotten.

RALPH. It makes it look like brown snow.

ANGELA. It looks odd when I put the sledges on, like the snow's gone brown so I've been thinking perhaps I should get rid of the sledges and what-have-you and just put cherries and almonds on. But then it's not as Christmassy and Eddie will be disappointed.

RALPH. He won't be disappointed.

ANGELA. He might be.

RALPH. He's thirty-five.

ANGELA. He pretends not to care, but he does, he wants everything the same. He's been like that since he was little.

RALPH. You're going to a lot of trouble. He ought to be grateful.

ANGELA. Let's not have any ructions.

RALPH. There won't be any ructions.

Not unless he makes them.

ANGELA. I just want us all to have a lovely time.

RALPH. Saying it won't make it happen.

ANGELA. So, anyway, what do you think? Go for the sledges or play safe with cherries and almonds?

Ralph? What do you think? What would you prefer?

RALPH. I don't mind.

ANGELA. It's not against the law to express a preference.

RALPH. Play safe then.

ANGELA. What, cherries and almonds? All right.

Be more of a standard fruitcake then.

Less of a Christmas cake as such.

I could do that.

It is a bit boring though.

RALPH. Then do the other.

ANGELA. All right. They were my mother's, some of those decorations. The little boy on the sledge and the girl skating. We had them during the war. No cake to put under them but there you are. It feels a bit funny not to use them.

RALPH. Then use them.

ANGELA. What?

RALPH. If you want to use them, then use them. Put the sledges on. It's not complicated.

ANGELA. Well now you're not helping!

RALPH. What do you want me to say?

ANGELA. I want you to express your true opinion!

RALPH. My true opinion?

ANGELA. Yes.

RALPH. My true opinion is that I don't care.

ANGELA. That's not very nice.

RALPH. My true opinion is that I don't care what you put on the cake.

ANGELA. I find that sad.

RALPH. I mean I don't mind either way.

ANGELA. That's not what you said.

> RALPH *is still working away on opening the first tea chest.*

> I don't want Eddie to be disappointed. That's all.

> *She sees an old slide projector tucked away in a corner.*

> I didn't know we still had that! Does it still work?

RALPH. What?

ANGELA. The slide thing! The thing we used to do the slide shows on! Does it still work?

RALPH. I've no idea.

ANGELA. And what about the slides? All those ones of Llangollen and the kids on the beach and those years when we had snow in Constable Court – I haven't seen them in years. Have we still got them?

5

RALPH. I don't know.

ANGELA. We'd still have them wouldn't we? We wouldn't have thrown those out. Surely not.

RALPH. I don't know. I might have.

ANGELA. Would they be up in the loft if we had them?

RALPH. I expect so.

ANGELA. We could have a look couldn't we – perhaps when –

RALPH. Not now.

ANGELA. Of course not now. When you've got a minute. When we put the decorations box back.

Or some other time. When we're less –

Perhaps it's not such a good idea. Bit boring for Catherine maybe. Poor girl doesn't want to see all our old, other people's memories, not very exciting.

Another time.

RALPH. I think I've nearly got this – can you pass me the –

ANGELA. But that box still needs to go back up, it's too big to be cluttering up the sitting room. There won't be room, especially when we get the folding bed out for Eddie and Catherine. Because we won't want to have to go up and down the stairs with it, putting it away every night – I thought perhaps if we moved the piano out a bit then the bed could slide in behind – though now with the tree up, I don't know if there's room – Oh, shoot, I haven't wiped it down, I meant to wipe that folding bed down before they got here, it's bound to be dusty. I'd better do it now. When are they coming for the – ? No. Cake first, get that sorted, then wipe the bed. I'd love to get that slide thing inside. It's probably quite heavy isn't it. Get Eddie to give us a hand maybe. Why those all have to come out of the boxes at all is beyond me, not when they're going to go straight into the boot of a car.

RALPH. Angela – just hold this, would you? – It's nearly coming, I don't want to –

ANGELA. Are there nails?

RALPH. Not if you hold it –

ANGELA. There is – there's a nail – Careful, Ralph, you nearly got me –

RALPH. No, I didn't – The nail is there, look, there it is –

ANGELA. Be careful, Ralph –

RALPH. I am being careful –

ANGELA. I don't think my tetanus is up to date, I don't think it's very safe to be –

RALPH. If you just hold onto it there, I can –

ANGELA. My aunt got tetanus off a rosebush, I'd better get my gloves on –

RALPH. Just take it – or I'm going to – !

ANGELA. Ow!

She reels back, clutching her hand.

RALPH. It's a scratch, it's just a tiny –

ANGELA. That hurt – you hurt me – you –

RALPH. If you hadn't made such a fuss –

ANGELA. I told you to be careful!

RALPH. I'm sorry.

ANGELA. You never have any patience and this is what happens –

RALPH. I'm sorry.

ANGELA. You have no patience!

RALPH. Sorry.

ANGELA. That needs Savlon now. Let's hope it won't need stitches. God knows how long you'd wait in casualty this time of year –

RALPH. It won't need stitches –

ANGELA. How do you know?

RALPH. I can tell –

ANGELA. Have you looked?

RALPH. I can see –

ANGELA. Why do you always have to rush things and ruin them? Why can't you just be patient? I've got cooking to do, and washing up, and all sorts of housework, the last thing I need is a wound to attend to –

RALPH. I've said I'm sorry.

ANGELA. And that's dangerous leaving all those nails sticking out like that.

RALPH. No one's going to touch them.

ANGELA. You should bang them down and make that edge safe or there'll be another accident.

RALPH. Who's going to touch them? No one's going to come near them.

Exit ANGELA.

Come on, let's have a look at the . . .

He's over at the now-open tea chest. Picks out a bundle wrapped in newspaper.

He turns and sees that she has gone.

He unwraps the bundle.

It is a carved wooden lamb.

He sets it on the ground. Sits back on his hunkers and drinks in the sight of it.

Oh, my darling. My darling boy.

Angela?

He crawls over to the slide projector. Drags it to the wall and finds a socket. He plugs it in and switches it on.

It whirs and a light comes on, throwing a square of light onto the opposite wall.

RALPH *finds the switch that makes the slides change and he switches it a few times. There are no slides in the carousel so the square of light remains just a blank square of light. He switches it a bit more; wipes away cobwebs; finds a cloth and gives it a little spit and a polish, switching as he goes.*

Suddenly a picture comes up. It is of a young man in a garage at a party in a CND T-shirt, aged eighteen. Clothes and hair indicate late eighties (in fact 1987). He has a cigarette and is laughing into the camera. This is Richard.

RALPH *stares.*

EDDIE *appears in the doorway, wearing big coat.*

RALPH *sees him, jumps, switches off the machine.*

EDDIE. Please God don't tell me we're having a slide show.

RALPH. No, no, your mother – (*Waves uncertainly.*) When did you get here?

EDDIE. Just now.

RALPH. Good journey?

RALPH *continues unpacking the case and unwrapping carved wooden sheep, cows, donkeys etc. through the following:*

EDDIE. Fine.

RALPH. Your mother thought it might be nice.

EDDIE. We'll look forward to that then.

RALPH. I must come and say hello to Catherine.

EDDIE. Cat?

RALPH. Yes.

EDDIE. Think she's having a piss.

Freshening up.

RALPH. Come by boat again did you?

EDDIE. Yes we did.

RALPH. She drove you did she?

EDDIE. Yup.

RALPH. All the way down from Holyhead?

EDDIE. Yup.

RALPH. That's a long drive.

EDDIE. Yup.

RALPH. You learning?

EDDIE. Nope.

RALPH. Thinking of starting?

EDDIE. No. Not really. I don't approve of driving.

RALPH. Driving's useful.

EDDIE. Yes, but then so is having a planet to live on.

RALPH. She must be tired doing all that driving.

EDDIE. I said let's take the train – she insisted. What can you do?

Having a clear out?

RALPH. They're for The Greyhound.

EDDIE. The Greyhound?

RALPH. Down by the station. Some woman rang up –

EDDIE. Who?

RALPH. I don't know, some girl or other, said she remembered them. Did we have them tucked away somewhere. So I thought, well, if it's for the local community –

EDDIE. But you hate the local community.

RALPH. It'll be in the bistro-restaurant bit.

EDDIE. Oh, well then. If it's for the bistro.

RALPH. It's meant to be quite good these days. The *Chronicle* gave it four stars the other week. So your mother says.

EDDIE. I didn't know you were interested in restaurants.

RALPH. We're not.

EDDIE. Didn't think so.

RALPH. Paying out for food you'd eat cheaper at home.

EDDIE. That's the spirit.

RALPH. I just don't see the point.

EDDIE. No, there is no point, you're right. (*Picking up a sheep.*) This is a good one.

RALPH. Do you think?

EDDIE. Nice expression.

RALPH. I think that was one of mine. Not sure.

So. What are you doing for money these days?

EDDIE. How do you mean?

RALPH. I mean, what are you doing for money?

EDDIE. Same old stuff. Walking the dogs. Sponging off the state. Don't want to break a family tradition. We finished the album. I think it's quite good actually, we've got a new –

RALPH. How about Catherine?

EDDIE. She's supply teaching. Making a fortune. Keeping me in the manner to which I've become accustomed.

RALPH. I thought she had a proper job at that school – hadn't they made her permanent or something?

EDDIE. She chucked it in. They were animals. Drinking, swearing, sniffing glue.

RALPH. Terrible.

EDDIE. And that was just the teachers.

RALPH. Isn't supply teaching even worse?

EDDIE. Well, Cat says at least you can go in with all guns blazing and then make a swift exit before they find out where you live.

RALPH *unwraps a donkey.*

They both look at it.

Is someone going to come and collect them?

RALPH. They're coming over with a car.

EDDIE. When?

RALPH. Any minute. We could start shifting them into the house. Your mother'll want to wipe them down or something. I'd better go and ask her.

You could start opening the next one, if you like.

EDDIE. All right.

RALPH. Look at that.

Can't teach that, that kind of delicacy. That kind of restraint. That's got to be in you, I think.

EDDIE. Yes, but then.

The road of excess leads to the palace of wisdom.

We hope.

Or I'm fucked.

RALPH. What?

EDDIE. Nothing.

RALPH *picks up the donkey and the sheep and leaves.*

EDDIE goes to the slide projector. Switches it on. The photograph of Richard comes up.

He stares at it for a bit.

Presses the switch – blank square.

He presses again and another slide comes up. Richard at the same party with his arm round a girl. She is wearing a bright pink fringed scarf.

EDDIE keeps switching the switch.

Bright-pink-scarf party-girl looking through her fingers captured in adolescent beauty.

More slides of a party, 1987. Richard with CND T-shirt.

He presses again and another picture of Richard and the girl – same party, now Richard's wearing the pink scarf. They are kissing.

EDDIE contemplates this picture for a while.

Then switches off the slide projector.

He opens the next tea chest.

Pulls out package and unwraps it.

It's the manger.

Enter KIRSTY.

KIRSTY. Hiya.

EDDIE. Hallo. Hi. Oh my God.

KIRSTY. Made you jump.

EDDIE. Yeah, you did. God. Kirsty.

KIRSTY. All right?

EDDIE. Yeah. How are you?

KIRSTY. Yeah. Fine.

They wonder whether to do a social kiss.

They don't.

EDDIE. Blimey.

KIRSTY. You all right?

EDDIE. Fine. Just. Didn't expect to see you. Jesus. What are you doing here?

KIRSTY. Your mum said to come and have a look. See if we want to take them all or not.

EDDIE. So was it you who rang up?

KIRSTY. Yes that was me, yes, did your dad say? Yes, because – well, we were a bit low on decorations and we needed something special for Christmas Day for the restaurant because we're really going for it this year, and we've got loads of bookings – and then – they just popped into my head, the crib scene your dad made, that was up in school, and I thought if they're still hanging around somewhere it'd be so much nicer than having loads of tat from B&Q, so I just thought –

EDDIE. I don't know, loads of tat from B&Q is very much in the spirit of the season.

KIRSTY. – I remembered that talk your dad did in assembly about the wood and the knives he used and how he made them and all that.

EDDIE. Oh God, yes, we were all as proud as Punch.

KIRSTY. Really?

EDDIE. No, not that I can recall.

KIRSTY. I still really like them.

EDDIE. I have to say you've hardly aged at all.

KIRSTY. Thank you.

Wish I could say the same about you.

EDDIE. It's been a tough couple of decades. So you still live here then?

KIRSTY. No, God, no, I mean yes, but it's temporary. I've been away, in London for ages but I broke up with someone. We were together for nine years, and living together and – it was all a bit – bleughh –

EDDIE. Right.

KIRSTY. And my dad's always said there's a job for you in the restaurant if you want it so I thought I might as well give it a go. Because my mum hasn't been up to much really since the operation. So I moved back in – the end of September.

Got my old bedroom back in fact.

EDDIE. And how is that?

KIRSTY. Great. Yes. Unbelievable. Still. At least this time I get the top bunk. And I'm saving up to buy.

And I quite like the bistro side of it, you can experiment a bit.

How about you these days? Are you – ?

EDDIE. I'm living in Dublin. Been there a while. With Cat. My girlfriend.

KIRSTY. Catherine I met just now?

EDDIE. Yup.

KIRSTY. She seems really nice.

EDDIE. She is really nice. Yes.

KIRSTY. How long have you been together?

EDDIE. Eight years.

KIRSTY. Kids?

EDDIE. No.

Pause.

KIRSTY. Do you get over quite often?

EDDIE. No, no – I don't . . . I'm busy and . . . I don't drive. And I don't want to.

KIRSTY. What are you up to?

EDDIE. Just stuff. Made a new album.

KIRSTY. Wow. So you're in a band.

EDDIE. Yes.

KIRSTY. That's amazing.

EDDIE. No, it isn't really, it's just this, it's just a – thing we've been working on –

KIRSTY. When are we going to see you on the telly?

EDDIE. I don't know. I don't know.

KIRSTY. Brilliant. What sort of music is it?

EDDIE. Sort of – indie-ethnic-pop, with a sort of . . . I don't know really.

KIRSTY. And what's it called, the band?

EDDIE. Supine.

KIRSTY. Soup – ?

EDDIE. Supine.

KIRSTY. Interesting.

EDDIE. We had to settle for that because we couldn't agree on anything else.

KIRSTY. Supine.

EDDIE. It was meant to suggest – being laidback. Or perhaps a bit lounge-lizardy. Sexually exhausted.

KIRSTY. Right.

Pause. KIRSTY *goes over and inspects the slide projector.*

We had one of these. Is it still working?

EDDIE. I don't know if it –

She switches it on and the picture of Richard kissing the girl in the pink scarf comes up.

She switches it off.

It's okay.

KIRSTY. Sorry.

EDDIE. It's all right. Put it on if you like.

Switch it on.

KIRSTY. Sorry, I shouldn't go round –

EDDIE. It's fine. Switch it on.

She switches it on.

They both look at the picture.

Look at that. Langered, the pair of them.

KIRSTY. What does that mean?

EDDIE. Drunk.

KIRSTY. You've got really Irish.

EDDIE. Really?

KIRSTY. What is she wearing?

EDDIE. More to the point, what is he wearing?

KIRSTY. CND.

EDDIE. All that marching up and down.

KIRSTY. Nicola was really into them. She used to get through a bottle of hairspray every two days.

EDDIE. So that was your sister then was it? Single-handedly destroying the ozone layer.

KIRSTY. It's not called that any more.

EDDIE. Isn't it?

KIRSTY. Anyway she had to maintain her look.

EDDIE. Of course she did.

What's she doing these days?

KIRSTY. Civil Service. They fast-tracked her after uni. She was always so brainy. I don't even know what she does. She's got this flat near Camden, lucky cow, bought it years ago. Worth a fortune. It's all minimal. Hardly anything in there. Just this enormous telly.

EDDIE. Sounds good. Is she – Is there a man on the scene?

KIRSTY. Not really. Not for ages. It's so weird being back in our old room. All our old crap is still in there. We were talking the other day actually. She mentioned Richard.

EDDIE. What did she say?

KIRSTY. She said. Not a day goes by that I don't think of him.

She's thirty-nine in February.

EDDIE. Is she panicking?

KIRSTY. She's not the panicking type.

EDDIE. I guess forty comes to us all.

Unless it doesn't.

He switches off the slide projector.

Shall we check out the rest?

EDDIE *passes out wrapped-up figures and* KIRSTY *unwraps them – sheep, cows, a calf.*

KIRSTY. Where's Mary and Joseph?

EDDIE. They must be in that one.

EDDIE *sets about prising the lid off the third box.*

Because now I remember there was some debate about it – because at first Richard didn't want any people, he wanted all animals.

KIRSTY. Why did he not want people?

EDDIE. He wanted it to be in the barn just before the humans arrived. But then Dad said there had to be a Baby Jesus. And Richard said, all right, have the Baby but what if Mary and Joseph had just gone outside to look at the stars for a minute and the Baby was there on its own.

But Dad overruled him. So there was definitely the three of them.

They manage to open the box. EDDIE pulls out two figures and unwraps the newspaper. Mary and Joseph.

That seems to be it.

KIRSTY. Shall I take them in then?

EDDIE. There is a Baby Jesus. Richard did it, I remember. It must be here somewhere –

KIRSTY. Not to worry. We can always – find a little doll or something.

EDDIE. But there definitely was one.

KIRSTY. We'll improvise. It's okay.

EDDIE. It's here though, it must be, it's just – hiding somewhere.

KIRSTY. I'll take these anyway.

KIRSTY takes the sheep, cows and calf, and leaves.

Mary and Joseph are lying on the floor.

EDDIE keeps looking around for the Baby Jesus – in all three boxes, in the pile of unwrapped newspaper.

Enter RALPH.

RALPH. Lost something?

EDDIE. I'm looking for Jesus.

RALPH. Is it not here then?

EDDIE. Haven't seen Him so far.

RALPH. Must be in one of the boxes. There was a Baby for the manger, definitely.

EDDIE. I know. But I've unpacked all the boxes and it's not there.

RALPH. Must be among this stuff. Or fell out when you unpacked Mary. I might have put those two wrapped up together or something.

EDDIE. Did He get left out? When you packed them up? Is He some-where else?

RALPH. No. I'd have kept the set together. It could have dropped out and rolled under here when you – Is it in that newspaper?

EDDIE. No, I've gone through it. It's not here.

RALPH. Just have a look would you?

EDDIE. I've looked, Dad.

RALPH. Then where is it?

EDDIE. We can keep looking. Maybe it got stuck up in the loft or something. Or with the Christmas decorations.

RALPH. No. We get that blinking box out every year, we'd have come across it if it was in there. Dammit. I knew I should have unpacked them myself. Your mother kept me hanging on –

EDDIE. I unpacked all the boxes and it wasn't in there.

RALPH. It might have fallen out when you weren't looking –

EDDIE. I was looking and it didn't.

RALPH. It's probably rolled underneath something –

EDDIE. Dad. It wasn't in the boxes or I'd have unpacked it. Okay?

RALPH. All right. All right.

I knew I should have done the job myself.

Idiot.

Never pays to try and cut corners, never.

Better get this stuff tidied up anyway.

EDDIE. You didn't say it was Kirsty who rang up.

RALPH. Who's Kirsty?

EDDIE. Kirsty Ellis. The girl from The Greyhound. Nicola's sister.

RALPH. Oh. Right. No, well, I didn't – register. I wouldn't have known the name. It was such a big school, I wouldn't have known –

EDDIE. Yes, but Kirsty, Nicola's sister, I'd have thought –

RALPH. Yes, right. Oh I see. I remember her now, it's just on the phone I didn't – didn't think it would be her.

Anyway – so I've met your Cat. Finally.

EDDIE. Good.

RALPH. She seems very nice.

EDDIE. She is.

RALPH. Good-looking girl.

EDDIE. Yup.

RALPH. When are you getting married?

EDDIE. I don't know. This year, next year, sometime –

RALPH. Can't carry on fornicating for the rest of your life.

Need to get yourself sorted.

You're no teenager any more. Are you?

There was this film on the other day and they had this song: 'It's later than you think, It's later than you think.' I thought, yes.

You listening?

EDDIE. Yes.

RALPH. Am I right?

EDDIE. I don't want to talk about it.

RALPH. Can't close your eyes for ever, drifting and dabbling. Walking dogs. What's that?

EDDIE. I don't –

RALPH. It's an insult to your education. An insult to your mother and me. An insult to all the chances and opportunities –

EDDIE. Don't go down this road, I don't want to go down this road.

RALPH. If you never start on anything, you'll never finish anything. The danger is you'll wake up and find your hair's gone grey.

EDDIE. It already has, Dad, can't you see?

RALPH. You need to decide. Keep this girl hanging on, paying your way for you, it's not –

EDDIE *picks up the manger, Mary and Joseph.*

EDDIE. See you later.

RALPH. Where are you going? Hey?

EDDIE *leaves, crashing into* TOM *as he does so.*

TOM. Hallo. I came to help with the rest of the –

EDDIE. It's all right, I've got them. They're all done.

TOM. Oh.

EDDIE looks at slide projector.

EDDIE. And I'm not touching that thing so don't even ask me.

Exit EDDIE.

TOM. Sorry, I, I, I –

RALPH. Take no notice of him, Tom, he's just . . . We had a little altercation. It's all right.

RALPH *starts to sweep and tidy up.*

TOM. All right.

RALPH. You happy with the crib then? Think it'll pass muster?

TOM. 'Pass muster' – ?

RALPH. Do the job. Look okay.

TOM. Look okay, yes. I think it's very okay, very nice, very nice, looks good. It's going to look good.

RALPH. Good to give them an airing. Set it all up how it was meant to be.

TOM. Tonight, Kirsty said, we'll do it tonight. After closing time.

RALPH. Perhaps we could come and have a look at it later on, have a little Christmas Eve drink or something, me and Angela, maybe Eddie and his girlfriend – would that be – ?

TOM. Yes, have a drink, maybe, Kirsty, I'll tell Kirsty, tell her you're coming. Drinks on the house!

RALPH. No need for that, we're not really drinking types. Anyway, we'll pay, we can pay.

TOM. Pay, okay.

RALPH. I'd better check with Angela if she wants that thing brought in. The slide projector.

Could you hang on for a minute and give me a hand if she wants it brought through?

TOM. All right, all right.

RALPH. I'll be back in a minute.

RALPH *leaves.*

TOM *goes over to the slide projector and switches it on.*

The slide of Richard's face comes up on the wall.

TOM *looks at it. Puts his hand in front of the beam, and then his face, so that the picture of Richard is projected onto his face. Then he presses the switch and the carousel moves on. Blank squares of light.*

More blank squares.

RALPH *has returned. He stands and looks at* TOM *for a second.*

Blackout.

Scene Two

The sitting room of a modest suburban semi-detached house in the south of England.

The same time of the same day.

ANGELA *enters, carrying the coat from Scene One.*

Her hand is bleeding.

She tries to control her breathing.

Ring at the doorbell. ANGELA *goes to answer it.*

Greetings, voices etc. offstage.

Enter EDDIE, *wearing a big coat and hat of some kind.*

He goes over and inspects the cake and decorations. Chucks his hat onto a sofa.

EDDIE. Your snow's gone brown.

ANGELA (*offstage*). Sorry, dear?

EDDIE. Where's Dad?

ANGELA (*offstage*). In the garage. He's sorting out the Nativity carvings.

ANGELA *enters.*

I just spiked my hand on one of the – He's always rushing at things, he's got no patience, he got me with a nail –

EDDIE. What happened to the cake?

ANGELA. Yes, I know, it's a pain isn't it – And Dad said it happened last year, I must have made the same mistake and it went clean out of my head – Do come through and warm up, Catherine, you must be –

Enter CAT.

– yes, such a pain, Dad said I did exactly the same thing last year and I completely forgot and did it all over again.

CAT. What's that?

EDDIE. Brown snow on the cake.

ANGELA. I was trying to avoid artificial colourings and e-numbers in a bid to be more healthy but –

EDDIE. It certainly has a kind of wholemeal ambience. Which I'm sure is bound to counteract the fat, sugar and lard content. Where did you say Dad was?

ANGELA. There's no lard in it. He's out in the garage. When did I ever put lard in a cake? He's sorting out the Nativity carvings, I told you.

EDDIE. Why?

ANGELA. You remember, the crib scene, with all the animals, the ones Dad and Richard made –

EDDIE. Yes I do remember them, but why is he – ?

ANGELA. Can I get you a cup of tea or anything, Catherine?

EDDIE. You're not chucking them out are you?

ANGELA. No, no, they're being organised for the – are you warm enough dear? – I don't know, I put that heating on but it's – No, we only got the tree up yesterday, and your father's landed himself with another job to do, as if we hadn't enough – We can put the heating up another notch, that might help, mightn't it –

CAT. No, no, I'm really warm thanks.

ANGELA. Did you say you would like tea? The kettle's just boiled.

CAT. Oh yes, please, that would be nice.

ANGELA *exits to make tea.*

ANGELA (*offstage*). Eddie? Cup of tea?

EDDIE. No thanks, I think I might go and see what Dad's up to.

ANGELA (*offstage*). Sugar for you, Catherine?

CAT. Half a spoon please.

ANGELA (*offstage*). Half?

CAT. Yes please.

EDDIE. Catch you later, Mater.

ANGELA (*offstage*). Sorry?

EDDIE. Don't show me up in front of the visitors.

EDDIE *leaves*.

ANGELA *comes back with tea at some point during the following*.

ANGELA. How was the drive?

CAT. It wasn't too bad actually, I was quite surprised.

ANGELA. Did you stop off?

CAT. Yes, several times. Eddie had a couple of fried breakfasts.

ANGELA. It's a shame he can't share the driving with you.

CAT. I don't mind really.

ANGELA. And how is your work going?

CAT. It's fine thank you. Busy, you know, Christmas, lots of sick people around . . . Did Eddie tell you I was back doing supply teaching?

ANGELA. Not your proper – Not the job you had before?

CAT. St Joseph's, no, no, I left there in the summer actually – I decided –

ANGELA. That's a shame.

CAT. No, no, it's – it was too much for me. The children were – It's a very deprived area and I just couldn't – I found the whole thing very –

ANGELA. Were they very rough?

CAT. They could be. And then – they came in with all sorts of problems and . . .

Sometimes you just feel so useless.

ANGELA. Oh dear –

CAT. And – then, the term before last, it was the final straw really– there was this one little girl in my class, Aisling, and she came from the flats, the estate near us, anyway we found out that she was –

ANGELA. That's a shame. So you're back doing the temporary –

CAT. Supply. It's fine. But I'm beginning to rethink teaching. I'm not sure if it's really me.

ANGELA. I often thought if I hadn't had the boys I might have gone into teaching.

CAT. Really?

ANGELA. Eddie's dad ended up in teaching, before he got ill, so I always knew about the downside. But I wouldn't have done secondary. It was the littlies I loved really.

CAT. Yes, they are great.

ANGELA. I used to love popping into the school. Even the smell of it, I liked. And the pictures up on the walls and the lovely beeswax polish on the floors and the books in the library. Amelia-Anne and the green umbrella. *Topsy and Tim*. I used to help with the swimming, with the infants, help them get their things on and off, and hear them read. And make cakes for the Christmas fair and all of that.

She fishes around in the decorations box and pulls out some children's notebooks.

I found these up in the attic, things the children wrote. I was going to show Ralph but –

This one: 'The beaver is a funny animal. He lives with his family in a lodge.'

CAT. 'How fish fingers are made.'

ANGELA. 'Once there was a princess she was very fond of music every year the potters brought their vases to see which one played the best music.'

CAT. Surreal.

ANGELA. These are all Eddie, I think.

CAT. Really?

ANGELA. Aged seven.

'War and Weapons – World War II Allied Aircraft. Handley Page Halifax Mk 11 Series 1 1911 could carry 13,000lb of bombs and fly at 285 miles per hour.'

Where's –

I had some of Richard's here somewhere.

His were mostly pictures.

CAT. This is good.

'What is a home?

A home is a safe place. It keeps out the rain and wind. It has plenty of windows so you can see out from a warm room. Inside you need lights. It's important to have your things about, with wallpaper you like and your furniture.

It is a place to come back to after the day. That you know is full of things you like, where there is food and drink. It's where you feel you belong. It's a small place that's different to all the other houses in the world.'

ANGELA. That was Richard.

Pause.

So what will you do if you give up teaching?

CAT. I thought maybe – interior design. Or – maybe – midwifery. But I'm not sure.

ANGELA. That sounds interesting.

CAT. I don't really know at this stage. I'm sort of – casting around.

ANGELA. Delivering babies.

CAT. Apparently there's a shortage.

ANGELA. Of babies or midwives?

CAT. Both, apparently.

ANGELA. I always wanted three. But Ralph said we couldn't afford it. It's funny the way men always make out they're so keen to procreate, programmed to drop their trousers and make babies at the least opportunity. In my experience they're always extremely reluctant.

CAT. Yes.

ANGELA. Or is that just with their wives?

CAT. I don't really know.

ANGELA. Of course nowadays there's lots of women happy to stay childless.

CAT. I suppose choosing to be child-free is something –

ANGELA. Child-free, is that the term these days?

CAT. I think sometimes –

ANGELA. It's so sad that nowadays people seem to regard children as a burden rather than a gift.

CAT. Yes.

Yes, that is sad.

> 'Thank you for the wind's strength
> Thank you for the whiteness of snow
> Thank you for the sun and rain
> That grows your gift of grain
> Thank you for the moon and stars
> O maker of weather
> Keep us all for ever and ever.'

Is this Eddie?

Or – ?

ANGELA. Life plays such tricks on you. You run around trying to fit the babies in between all the other things you think you want, and then, years later, you realise the thing you were desperately trying to contain and minimise, turns out to be probably the only important thing you'll ever do.

If you're lucky.

CAT. I guess lots of things are important though, aren't they?

ANGELA. I'm only giving my opinion, I know people don't agree with me.

And then if you're unlucky – all you have to show for it might be some crayon and a scrap of paper.

CAT. But surely you don't think that.

ANGELA. What do you mean?

CAT. About Richard?

ANGELA. I think he stumbled out into the night and we lost him. All he was, all he could ever be.

CAT. But he hasn't gone from your mind. And the people who knew him.

ANGELA. I don't know. I don't know. I've done my best. To do right by him. Because one way or another they all left me, the menfolk,

Ralph's heart broke, literally broke, the heart attacks, that's why he had to take his early retirement. And Eddie went away as soon as he could, years together we barely saw him, not even at Christmas. So it was me that had to do – what needed to be done.

CAT. What needed to be done?

ANGELA. They're telling me it's an accident. That a boy who is eighteen years old, who never drank, who was always extremely careful crossing the road, who'd been using that cyclepath and the level crossing since he was twelve, that he could just walk out under a train like that. It's not credible, it doesn't make sense. People don't just die like that. They don't. It's on somebody's conscience. Somebody knows. There should have been safety mechanisms in place on that crossing – and they know it. It's just finding the evidence.

CAT. What sort of evidence?

ANGELA. There were plans in place for a review of safety procedures going back to 1985, it's there in the minutes of the Council in black and white, and I've been trying to find out why they never went ahead. And even just a few weeks ago – there was a letter came through from the –

Doorbell rings.

This must be them. Ask me about this later because I can show you the –

She goes to answer the door. Sounds perhaps of greetings etc.

ANGELA *re-enters with* KIRSTY *and* TOM.

TOM *carries a wooden box with a slot at the front for posting letters through.*

We're all at sixes and sevens I'm afraid – my husband's just out the back, he's sorting out the boxes – He's unpacking them all, I told him they could go straight into the car but he insisted –

TOM. Hullo.

CAT. Hullo.

KIRSTY. Hi there.

CAT. Hi, I'm Eddie's –

ANGELA. We have visitors, you see, this is Catherine, Eddie's partner, and this is – I'm sorry, what were your names again – ?

KIRSTY. Kirsty. Kirsty Ellis.

ANGELA. Kirsty. Oh. My goodness.

KIRSTY. My mum and dad run The Greyhound.

ANGELA. I hadn't twigged –

KIRSTY. Nicola, my sister, you probably remember –

ANGELA. Nicola's sister. From The Greyhound.

KIRSTY. Yes that's right. And I was at Our Lady's Grove –

ANGELA. You were Eddie's year, weren't you?

KIRSTY. Couple of years below. Nicola was the same year as –

ANGELA. Yes, of course, that's right, of course, I know you now, I remember Nicola, yes – Goodness, I didn't think, Ralph didn't – And your parents are still . . . ?

KIRSTY. Still at The Greyhound. This is Tom, my little brother. And commis chef.

TOM. Hullo.

ANGELA. Ralph said The Greyhound, but here was me thinking it must have changed hands by now. I saw it got four stars in the local rag, the bistro bit.

KIRSTY. Yes, we did, which was really nice. We've got loads of bookings for tomorrow, so the crib's going to make it really . . . Is Eddie about?

ANGELA. Yes, he's just in the – Out with his – Oh, here he comes – Ralph –

Enter RALPH *carrying the donkey and the sheep.*

Ralph, this is Kirsty and –

KIRSTY. Tom.

ANGELA. Kirsty and Tom from The Greyhound, Ralph, Nicola's sister, do you remember? If they need a wipe, Ralph, I'd rather they went on a plastic sheet – Can you hang on for a minute – Do you remember, Ralph, the Ellis girls from The Greyhound? Just shows how out of touch you can get. You know I said I thought it had changed hands, well it turns out not only was I wrong about that but Kirsty's still helping out in the kitchen –

KIRSTY. I'm managing the bistro.

ANGELA. Isn't that strange?

KIRSTY. It's temporary, obviously, I've been working in –

ANGELA. Course we realised it had to be somebody from the school who remembered the crib scene and so on but I just never made that connection, did you, Ralph?

Not on the carpet – Just hang on for me a minute will you?

KIRSTY. Thank you for lending them.

RALPH. You're welcome. About time we let them see the light of day again.

ANGELA. And this is Tom. Kirsty's brother.

And this of course, last but not least, is Catherine.

RALPH. Eddie's dad.

CAT. I thought you might be.

RALPH. Ralph.

CAT. Catherine. Or just Cat.

RALPH. Very pleased to meet you.

ANGELA. Right. Well how much more is there?

RALPH. There's three boxes, you saw them yourself. There's quite a few more.

ANGELA. Will you want all of them do you think? Eddie's still out there, you could pop out and have a look. Because if you don't want them all they can stay in the boxes and that'll be less mess in here.

KIRSTY. All right.

KIRSTY *leaves*.

RALPH. So we've finally managed to lure the pair of you across the water.

CAT. That's right.

RALPH. About time.

CAT. Yes, absolutely.

ANGELA. Don't put them on the carpet, Ralph, let me get the water-proof –

Exit ANGELA.

RALPH. Good journey?

CAT. Yes, it was fine, thanks.

RALPH *sets down the donkey and the sheep on the carpet.*

RALPH. Would you like a drink?

CAT. Are you having one yourself?

RALPH. Yes. I think I might. Drop of the Grouse, what do you say?

CAT. Go on then.

RALPH. Would you like it hot? Sugar – cloves – slice of lemon?

CAT. Sounds perfect.

RALPH. Tom? Drink for you? Whisky? Sherry? Beer?

TOM. No, no thanks, thank you, no thanks.

RALPH *exits to prepare drinks.*

CAT. What's that you've got there?

TOM. It's a wishbox. I made it, to go near the bar, for the customers, for Christmas wishes. You write your wish on a card and post it in there.

CAT. You've got quite a few then. And what's going to happen to them?

TOM. The wishbox gets opened on Christmas Eve at midnight and we read the letters out loud. And that makes them come true.

CAT. Of course. I like it. Sort of letters to Santy but for grown-ups.

TOM. Yes, yes, letters. Like letters to Santa.

CAT. And you made it yourself?

TOM. Yes.

CAT. Good job. It's very nice. So you're a carpenter too.

TOM. No, no – I help in the kitchen, at The Greyhound, help Kirsty in the bistro, sous chef, commis chef – chopping and I do the prep and . . . They want me to go to catering, catering, catering, do catering at college.

CAT. Catering college. That'll be good.

TOM. No, no, but, I don't want – It's not, it's not what I want to do, I want to – I want to – be – this – be a – carpenter.

CAT. Really?

TOM. Yes, yes but they, they, my parents, don't think – I could – They don't think because of the papers, paperwork, don't think I could be a carpenter because I would have to – to employ, employ, be –

CAT. Self-employed?

TOM. Yes. They think it's too hard. I couldn't, they don't think, even if I could do the carving I –

CAT. But couldn't someone help you with that?

TOM. Yes, you see, what I thought, I thought, I had this idea, I thought, what if I asked, what if I showed it to – if someone could recommend me –

Enter RALPH *with drinks.*

RALPH. Now.

CAT. Thank you.

RALPH. Eddie said you'd given up your job?

CAT. I've gone back to supply teaching, yes, I just – needed a break really.

RALPH. You were in that job a while though, weren't you?

CAT. St Joseph's? Yes, two years almost. Eighteen months.

RALPH. Teaching can be tough all right.

CAT. Yes. I had . . . I just had enough for a while. Angela said you were a teacher yourself?

RALPH. Was. Yes. CDT. That's what they called it back then. Craft, Design and Technology. In my case just a fancy name for –

TOM. Carpentry.

RALPH. Woodwork. Secondary school; Eddie's old school actually.

CAT. Oh, I see –

Enter ANGELA, *with plastic cloth and dusters.*

ANGELA. Ralph! I said to wait! Now there's muck all over the carpet!

RALPH. There isn't!

ANGELA. Why couldn't you wait? I asked you to wait!

RALPH. They're not dirty, Angela! They've been sealed in boxes and wrapped in newspaper – with the lids nailed down! / How could there be mess?

ANGELA. Always this rush and impatience and all you do is make more and more and more work for me –

RALPH. There's no mess. This isn't mess. For Christ's sake!

ANGELA. Oh, all right!

RALPH. I don't know why you have to be so hysterical about every-thing –

ANGELA. And I don't know why you have no patience and absolutely no compunction about keeping things clean / and making extra work when you know I've a million things to do at Christmas, what with visitors and cards –

RALPH. I keep things clean, I do keep things clean –

ANGELA. and yes, my hand does hurt, by the way, thanks very much for asking. I've just about staunched the flow but we'll all be lucky if I don't get tetanus! And if I do we'll know who's to blame!

RALPH. Where are you going?

ANGELA. Going to get that guest bed wiped down. All I get is criti-cism, criticism, criticism, all the time, pick, pick, pick, I'm sick of it! And all I'm trying to do is make things nice for everybody!

RALPH. No one's criticising you, Angela –

ANGELA. I'm sick of it!

She exits.

RALPH (*raising his glass*). Here's to Christmas. *Sláinte!*

CAT. *Sláinte!* (*Digs in her handbag, brings out a CD.*) We brought this. You'll have to have a listen.

RALPH. What is it?

CAT. It's the album. Eddie's new baby.

RALPH. What are they called again?

CAT. Supine.

RALPH *laughs grimly.*

RALPH. He wants to get himself a proper job.

CAT. Talking of jobs – Tom here was saying about wanting some career advice – weren't you? On the subject of carpentry. Was it Ralph you wanted to have a word with?

RALPH. Oh I don't give advice. Those days are over.

Enter ANGELA, *dragging a folding bed with her.*

ANGELA. Anyway, here I was thinking of this for the pair of you and when I opened it out just now, blow me if it isn't a single bed, I can't believe it –

CAT. Don't worry, Angela.

ANGELA. And I was so sure it was a double.

CAT. It's okay, we can squadge up.

ANGELA. I don't know how I got that in my head. Making all these stupid mistakes, what with this and the – It's all just turning into a bit of a disaster –

CAT. No, really, it's fine, Angela, we can . . .

RALPH. They can squadge. Listen to what the girl says. Or there's a bed upstairs in the spare room.

ANGELA. Yes I know, Ralph, but that's only a single bed, isn't it, and there's no room next to it on the floor for even a mattress. And I'd clear out the other room / if we had a couple of mattresses or something to go on the floor but it's my office and it's overflowing, we couldn't even –

RALPH. You should have a sort-out and chuck some of that paperwork away, I've always said so, I've been on at her for months –

ANGELA. I know, I know, I haven't had time, when have I had time to do a sort-out, anyway, they'd want to be together, wouldn't they, the pair of them, that's why I thought down here on the folding bed would have been perfect, but I obviously got it –

CAT. It's fine, honestly, one of us can just kip on the sofa.

ANGELA. I don't want you to be uncomfortable.

CAT. The sofa's fine. I like sofas.

ANGELA. We used to have that lilo. Ralph, where would the lilo be?

RALPH. That's no use, Angela.

ANGELA. It was a good lilo. We used it for years.

RALPH. I last saw that lilo in Llangollen 1976 and it was on its last legs even then.

ANGELA. Don't we still have it?

RALPH. No, and even if we did, the least said the better.

ANGELA. Are you drinking?

RALPH. Hot whisky. Do you want one?

ANGELA. Is that what you've got, Catherine?

CAT. I'm afraid it is, yes.

RALPH. We're hitting the Grouse and it's not yet 5 pm. Do you want one, Angela?

ANGELA. No, I don't thanks.

RALPH. Come on, it's Christmas.

ANGELA. I've got too much to do.

Enter KIRSTY *with sheep, cows and calf.*

How are you getting on? Will you want all of them, do you think?

KIRSTY. I think so, yes, if that's all right.

ANGELA. Look, you stay in here and keep warm. Ralph can get the rest – can't you, Ralph? He'll want to tidy up and sort the workshop out anyway. Put your coat on.

Exit RALPH.

So do you want them to go back in the boxes or – ?

KIRSTY. No, I think they'll fit better if we put them straight in the boot as they are . . .

ANGELA. Right. You two give them a dust-over with a damp cloth, and I'll go and see if I've got an old blanket somewhere, you don't want to get the edges bashed or –

Exit ANGELA.

The donkey, various sheep, cows and calf are all standing on the matting.

TOM *touches them.*

KIRSTY *and* CAT *pick up dusters and begin cleaning the carvings.*

CAT. So has he changed much since school – Eddie?

KIRSTY. No. He seems completely the same. He always said he was going to be in a band and famous.

CAT. He got it half right then.

KIRSTY. Does he do a lot of gigs and things over in Ireland?

CAT. Some.

KIRSTY. We used to be an item, actually, Eddie and me. Back in the old days.

CAT. Really?

KIRSTY. In fourth year. For about ten minutes. You know when you're fourteen.

CAT. I don't actually. It wasn't like that when I was fourteen. We had nuns.

KIRSTY. Full-on Catholic Irish stuff then?

CAT. Big time. Don't wear shiny patent shoes or the boys'll see your knickers in the reflection. That type of thing.

KIRSTY. Scary.

CAT. So you must have known Richard then?

KIRSTY. He went out with my sister.

CAT. Really?

KIRSTY. For ages.

Tom, can you go and see if there're any more figures to come out? These are done.

TOM. Done, okay, figures to come out. Where is it – ?

KIRSTY. Just out the back door and left along the patio and you'll see the garage door – It's open and the light's on.

Exit TOM.

So, yes, anyway, they were together ages. Richard and my sister.

CAT. How long?

KIRSTY. Two or three years, I think. Up until he died.

CAT. God. Your poor sister.

KIRSTY. But I don't think –

CAT. What?

KIRSTY. I don't think – Ralph and Angela. You know. I don't know. They didn't seem . . . I think they just thought – Oh, those girls from the pub, do you know what I mean? They weren't really –

Enter EDDIE, *holding the manger, Mary and Joseph.*

Sets them down on the floor.

EDDIE. Fucking arsehole.

CAT. Everything all right?

EDDIE. Lovely, thank you. When are we going home?

KIRSTY *and* CAT *start cleaning down the manger and then the figures.*

CAT. The day after Stephen's Day.

EDDIE. Boxing Day, not Stephen's Day, we're in Blighty, remember. Christ. Three whole nights?

CAT. Why is it Boxing Day?

EDDIE. Three nights. Oh, Christ. Can't we say we left the gas on?

CAT. You haven't answered my question.

EDDIE. What question?

CAT. Why do you call it Boxing Day?

EDDIE. I've no idea. And what the hell is that?

CAT. Our bed.

EDDIE. Our bed? We're not going to fit on there.

CAT. Your mum had it in her head it was a double.

EDDIE. Well it's clearly not. How does she expect us to sleep on that?

CAT. One of us can sleep on the sofa. Or apparently there's a single bed upstairs.

EDDIE. They can bloody well give us their bed.

CAT. Don't be stupid.

EDDIE. Why not? We're the guests. And they've obviously gone to zero effort to put us up.

CAT. Sssh.

EDDIE. I won't shush. It's pathetic. Years of nagging to come back for Christmas and they can't even be arsed to organise a proper place for us to sleep.

CAT. I'll sleep on the couch.

EDDIE. You will not. We'll check into a hotel.

CAT. Oh sure, right, okay.

EDDIE. I'm not joking. This pisses me off. This is so absolutely typical. She thinks she wants us to come and stay but she doesn't really. Really she has no interest in us being here or in actually welcoming us into her home.

CAT. Don't be silly.

EDDIE. As is made evident by her complete refusal to put in any actual effort or forethought in any way whatsoever . . .

CAT. Calm down, Ed.

EDDIE. I mean, what is so hard about even going and buying a folding bed for two people? Compared to the effort and cost of bringing a car across the Irish Sea? She likes the idea of us trekking bloody miles to visit her but she can't be arsed – neither of them can be arsed – to put in the merest bit of emotional or, God knows, financial effort to provide even the most basic levels of hospitality!

Look at this crap!

I slept on this when I was nine years old and it wasn't comfortable then!

What the hell is she thinking?

Enter ANGELA.

This wouldn't happen in a proper culture! It wouldn't happen in Ireland! In a proper culture there'd be a bit of bloody celebration. Killing the fatted calf and actually putting some effort into having your family around you. But not in England, oh no, that would be a bit too much like actually showing you cared about someone, not just going on, endlessly, about how much you miss your family, but actually doing something real and genuine to show that just very very occasionally you thought about their simple physical happiness! No that would be a little bit too real! Just a little bit too much like being joyful! Being present in the moment! Doing something real and actual and humble like providing a bed for someone even if it cost you the tiniest bit of expenditure – of your will, of your thought, of your money, of your –

Enter RALPH.

See – I'm even too afraid to say the word. See? I'm even too afraid to say the word – This fucked-up culture, this English thing, this miserable, joyless, tight-arsed fucking culture – I'm even too afraid to say the word love. That's what this is about – it's about a deep-seated fundamental lack of love! It's about an absence – a lacuna – a yearning fucking gaping chasm in all our hearts! And it's everywhere! It's hollowing us out! Perfect example: why is it called Boxing Day? I don't know! I bet no one in this room knows! It's just another fucking example. In Ireland they call it St Stephen's Day after the first Christian martyr so that simply by saying the name of the day you engage with the insane but beautiful notion that people through history have died in the name of Christ, have actually died by piercing and stoning and wounding and crucifixion for what they think is the glory of God and mad as the entire enterprise is at least it's not gift solutions and two-for-fucking-one at Boots and value Christmas at Tesco's and the whole performance we get dragged through year after year after bloody year; at least in Ireland they know why the day has the name it has! And there's blood and loss and sacrifice in it!

Like life.

Like life, underneath the anaesthetic of it all. Because what would happen if we unhooked ourselves from the epidural of our non-culture for just a few minutes? We'd feel the pangs! We'd remember again that what's really going on is unbelievably excruciating – and unbelievably messy – and unbelievably beautiful – If we let it – if we allowed ourselves actually to remember, to –

To feel.

RALPH. Do you still want that slide projector brought in?

ANGELA. Yes please, dear.

Blackout.

Scene Three

Later on, in the pub, after closing time.

The crib scene – with its empty manger – has been arranged.

The wishbox is on a little table nearby and it has a handwritten card-board sign next to it – 'Place Your Christmas Wish in Here!'– and a little pile of blank postcards.

CAT *sips her drink.*

After a minute she goes to get a postcard from the pile and gets a pen from her handbag.

She writes on the postcard.

She hides it as EDDIE *enters from the Gents.*

EDDIE. Still no sign of the paroids?

CAT. No.

EDDIE. Look, it's okay, Cat, I'm their son, they're used to me.

CAT. Yes.

EDDIE. They'll forgive me.

CAT. Will they?

EDDIE. They always do, it's their job. Anyway I was right.

CAT. Lots of people are right. It doesn't give you unlimited licence to behave like a complete arsehole.

EDDIE. No.

CAT. And to embarrass me.

EDDIE. I know.

CAT. It was a folding bed.

EDDIE. I know.

CAT. It was just a guest bed!

EDDIE. I know. I get . . .

CAT. I mean, Jesus!

EDDIE. Sorry.

I was right though.

What are you writing?

CAT. Nothing.

EDDIE. Do you want another drink?

CAT. No. Thanks. Driving.

EDDIE. Oh fuck it. Have another and we can walk back.

CAT. I don't want to.

EDDIE. Oh come on, it's only a couple of miles. Be a naughty devil. Have that muck you used to have, that mad old lady drink. What was it? Dubonnet and lemon!

What's the matter?

CAT. Nothing.

EDDIE. Don't make me have to woo you. What is it?

CAT. Really nothing.

EDDIE. Okay.

He picks up her wishcard. She swipes it off him.

He looks at her.

CAT. You're not supposed to read my wish.

EDDIE. Oh, you mean it won't work if I do?

CAT. It's private.

EDDIE. It's not really is it because if it's what I think it is, then it's going to have to involve me one way or another.

CAT. What do you mean?

EDDIE. Well, either I've got to co-operate, or –

CAT. Or what?

EDDIE. Or you've got to leave me.

CAT. God.

EDDIE. What?

CAT. I didn't know you saw it so starkly.

EDDIE. Well it's true, isn't it?

CAT. Jesus.

EDDIE. I'm not averse to . . .

CAT. What? Averse to what?

EDDIE. Facing this head-on.

CAT *laughs*.

What?

CAT. I thought for one delirious moment you were about to say you weren't averse to talking about this, or thinking about it, or . . .

EDDIE. I can talk. I can talk, if you want me to.

CAT. I just wish you could open your fucking mind.

EDDIE. My mind is open.

CAT. No it's not. You don't want babies.

EDDIE. That's right.

Neither did you.

Until quite recently.

CAT. And now I do.

EDDIE. Why?

CAT. I want to know what they'd be like.

I want people coming to me at Christmas. I want to be the grown-up.

EDDIE. That's not dependent on producing offspring.

CAT. No.

EDDIE. What's wrong?

CAT. I had this dream last night. About Aisling. I was reading this book with her and getting her to point to the words and at first it was normal. But then there started to be these horrible pictures. Every time we turned the page there was something worse. Awful things, just, knives, and blood, and – I don't even want to . . . I didn't want her to see them, I wanted to stop reading and close the book. But I didn't. I kept making her read.

EDDIE. You need to get over this.

CAT. Why? Why should we always permit ourselves to get over things?

EDDIE. You couldn't have known.

CAT. I could have. I should have made a phone call. I should have gone round there –

EDDIE. You could have done those things and it would have made no difference. It's just the world, it's just fate, they're up there, the old cronies, spinning the threads, and sometimes they're weaving some kind of mercy into the web –

CAT. Mercy.

EDDIE. – and sometimes they're not, and there's no second chances and there's nothing we can do about it –

CAT. I'm weak, I'm a sinner, I . . .

EDDIE. So am I, so am I, it's all of us, darling, all of us, not just you.

CAT. Do you not love me?

EDDIE. I do – do love you.

CAT. I want to see their faces.

EDDIE. Whose faces?

CAT. The faces of our –

EDDIE. I don't know where to go with this one.

CAT. Neither do I.

Why?

Why can't you even contemplate it?

Even to please me?

EDDIE. Because.

It's a vale of tears.

You have a baby. You love the baby, you would die for it. What then?

What happens when something goes wrong?

CAT. Why are you so frightened?

EDDIE. You should have babies.

CAT. Really?

EDDIE. I'd be crap at them. I'd screw them up. But you wouldn't. You'd be good.

CAT. Right.

EDDIE. If you want them you should have them. Lots of them.

CAT. Right. Just not with you?

What are you saying?

I have to leave you?

Jesus.

Grabs up the wishcard and is about to rip it up.

EDDIE *takes it off her and puts it into the wishbox.*

What did you do that for?

EDDIE. Take it to a higher power.

Let there be – an intervention.

CAT. From what? The elves?

EDDIE. Come on, let's get a drink.

CAT. I don't want to walk home.

EDDIE. The 'oids can drive. They're bringing the car.

CAT. What are we, teenagers?

Enter RALPH.

EDDIE. Where's Mum?

RALPH. She didn't fancy it.

EDDIE. Is she sulking?

RALPH. She's just – not a pub person.

EDDIE. It's Christmas Eve! They've just set the thing up! We're all having a little Christmas toast! How could she not fancy it?

RALPH. You know your mother.

EDDIE. What the hell is wrong with her?

Enter KIRSTY.

KIRSTY. So what can I get you?

RALPH. Pint of Broadside please. Catherine?

EDDIE. Did you come in the car, Dad?

RALPH. As it happens, I caught the bus.

EDDIE. Right.

RALPH. So I'm afraid I can't offer you a sober lift home. In fact I wondered if –

CAT. That's fine. I'm not drinking. I can drive, no problem. Just a – Coke please.

KIRSTY. Diet?

CAT. No.

RALPH. Thank you. We're not big drinkers, Ed's mother and me, I wouldn't normally – but given the circumstances, I thought . . . Eddie? What'll you have?

EDDIE. I'll have another Guinness. Thanks, Dad.

RALPH. You've done a good job there.

KIRSTY. Are you happy with it?

RALPH. It looks good. Shame about the Baby Jesus.

KIRSTY. We'll find something.

RALPH. You can't just have an empty manger.

KIRSTY. We can improvise.

RALPH. So are there many bookings for tomorrow?

KIRSTY. Yeah, not bad. Thirty covers odd. We've done quite well.

RALPH. This woman has to make thirty Christmas dinners.

KIRSTY. Not quite.

CAT. That's seriously impressive.

EDDIE. Cat struggles with toast.

CAT. Shut up.

RALPH. I'm sure Cat has other things to offer.

His mobile phone rings.

Excuse me.

He moves away and talks on the phone.

KIRSTY. That everything?

EDDIE. Yes, thanks.

Or will you have one yourself?

KIRSTY. I might do. Join you for a little while. Thanks.

EDDIE. And where's Tom?

KIRSTY. Kitchen. Prepping the veg. Might go and see how he's doing.

Exit KIRSTY.

EDDIE. No prizes for guessing who that might be on the phone. Haranguing him to return to his house arrest.

CAT. Oh, God.

EDDIE. What's the matter?

CAT. This doesn't feel like it's going brilliantly well.

EDDIE. I disagree. I'm having a simply lovely time.

CAT. Why are you so angry with your parents?

EDDIE. I'm not.

CAT. Yes you are.

EDDIE. I've forgiven. I've forgotten. I've moved on.

CAT. Do you think?

EDDIE. Yes I do think. I've moved as far west as you can go without going to America.

CAT. No you haven't.

EDDIE. What?

CAT. Meath is further west. Galway is further west. Many, many places are further west.

EDDIE. Let me clarify. As far west as you can go that isn't America and that isn't actually hell on wheels.

CAT. Moving away isn't the same as moving on.

EDDIE. I'm making a new life in another culture. A better one. A downtrodden one. Yours.

CAT. Why is it better?

EDDIE. Come on. You can't swagger round the globe, kicking the crap out of everyone you encounter, without fucking yourself up in the process.

If on the other hand, you never make any mistakes because you've never had the opportunity . . . or the guts – well –

KIRSTY *returns with tray of drinks.*

KIRSTY. Here we are. On the house.

CAT. That's funny, though, because I thought it was me you were making a new life with. Not just my downtrodden culture.

Or should that be my gutless culture?

EDDIE. Well it's both really. *Sláinte!*

CAT. Cheers! And *tiocfaidh àr là* [pronounced 'chuckie ar lar'] to you too!

EDDIE. Ah. How quaint and nostalgic that phrase sounds now. Even the old causes have lost their clout.

Enter RALPH, *reaching for his wallet.*

It's on the house, Dad.

RALPH. That's very kind. Are you sure?

KIRSTY. Of course.

RALPH. Well. Thank you. Cheers!

ALL. Cheers!

KIRSTY. And congratulations on your work.

RALPH. That's all long gone. Long over.

Pause.

EDDIE. What news?

RALPH. What?

EDDIE. Who was it?

RALPH. Your mother.

EDDIE. What did she want?

RALPH. I don't know.

EDDIE. The mobile phone. Wonderfully effective tool for communication.

CAT. She's not going to come out?

RALPH. She says it's too late for her.

EDDIE. No later than midnight mass.

RALPH. She doesn't like driving at night. Usually lets me do it. But I said tonight's one night I won't, I fancy a Broadside.

That's what set her off I think.

CAT. We could go and get her.

EDDIE. Oh, Jesus.

CAT. I mean, I could go and get her in the car. It's only a few minutes' drive.

RALPH. That's a thought.

CAT. Why don't I just go now and see if she'll come back with me?

RALPH. She sounded like she might be persuadable.

CAT. She'd like to see the crib, wouldn't she? Given the day that's in it?

RALPH. All right then. I'll come with you.

CAT. It's all right, you don't –

RALPH. No, I'll come. It's fine.

EDDIE. You sure you want to do this, Cat?

CAT. Sure.

RALPH. Mind my pint.

EDDIE. Will do.

RALPH. Back shortly.

EDDIE. Right you are.

CAT. See you later.

EDDIE. Drive carefully.

CAT and RALPH *leave.*

KIRSTY *and* EDDIE *sit and drink.*

Cheers!

KIRSTY. Cheers!

It's so weird to see you back here.

EDDIE. Yes, isn't it.

KIRSTY. I was telling Cat about us at school.

EDDIE. She said. That seems a hundred million years ago.

KIRSTY. Yes.

EDDIE. So, you're nursing a broken heart then?

KIRSTY. What can you do?

He took too much of my youth. Comes a time you have to say – *basta!*

EDDIE. *Basta* you bastard!

They smile at each other.

KIRSTY. You haven't changed.

EDDIE. God, don't say that.

KIRSTY. Still chasing all your – passions.

EDDIE. I don't know, don't know if I am.

Cat's the one really – teaching kids and – doing her best, and I'm just a – lazy stupid feckless arsehole. Basically.

KIRSTY. Harsh.

EDDIE. Truth hurts.

KIRSTY. You're a musician.

EDDIE. I'm nothing. I can't even live in my own country.

KIRSTY. Live where you want to.

EDDIE. Making nothing of any value. Passing on nothing of value. Disappearing like I was never there at all.

KIRSTY. Why should you make things? Why should you pass things on?

EDDIE. You make things.

KIRSTY. Yeah. *Bœuf* Stroganoff.

EDDIE. That's something. That's real. Feed people. That's good.

KIRSTY. It's not what I want.

EDDIE. What do you want?

> KIRSTY *can't answer.*

> God. We're a shower of losers aren't we? Genetically speaking. The fucking lost generation.

KIRSTY. How do you mean?

EDDIE. We're none of us teenagers. We're all of us in our thirties. And still not a kid to show between us. You, me, Cat. Your sister. Richard. Though I suppose he has an excuse.

KIRSTY. Perhaps you should drop a note in Tom's wishbox?

EDDIE. Oh, no. No, that's not me. That's Cat's thing. I'm not wishing for anything. Not now.

KIRSTY. Not ever?

EDDIE. I don't think so.

KIRSTY. But what about Cat?

EDDIE. What about her?

KIRSTY. What about what she wants?

EDDIE. What can I do?

KIRSTY. If you can't give her what she wants, then she'll leave. You'll lose her.

EDDIE. Then that'll be her decision, I guess.

KIRSTY. How can you be so passive about it?

EDDIE. Just my nature. I'm calm like the Buddha. Laid back.

KIRSTY. Like your band – what was it? Spineless?

EDDIE. Supine.

KIRSTY. Ah, right. The sexually exhausted lounge lizards.

EDDIE. I quite like Spineless.

KIRSTY. Men are unbelievable. I'm amazed there's a human race at all.

EDDIE. Well, probably soon there won't be. We'll all be flooded out, fried, boiled, frozen and then ripped apart by methane storms. Which kind of makes the big debate about – Golly, should I sacrifice my career to have a baby all seem kind of – academic. Big relief all round. Turn up the fucking thermostat.

KIRSTY. And you have another excuse to do absolutely nothing.

EDDIE. Not an excuse – that's science.

KIRSTY. Very convenient timing for you.

EDDIE. I just can't help seeing the bigger picture.

KIRSTY. But you've got a nice girlfriend.

EDDIE. I know.

KIRSTY. And she wants to have kids. And you're thinking about letting her go because you haven't got enough imagination to think – Hey, maybe having a child with someone I love might not be so terrible after all.

And yet here you are moaning you'll leave nothing behind you.

EDDIE. Nothing of value, I meant.

KIRSTY. People have no value.

EDDIE. They screw up, they break. They don't work properly. They die.

KIRSTY. Okay, so what does have value?

EDDIE. Music, maths, objects. Artefacts. Those, I like.

KIRSTY. Things you can control.

EDDIE. Yup.

KIRSTY. Anyway, as it happens, you're wrong. One of us has had a baby.

EDDIE. Who? What? You?

Have you?

KIRSTY. No. Not me. My sister.

EDDIE. What, lonely old Nicola?

KIRSTY. She had a baby.

EDDIE. The Civil Servant with the minimal flat in Camden? That Nicola?

KIRSTY. Yes.

EDDIE. What, so it's a minimal flat with baby sick?

KIRSTY. No. Not exactly.

EDDIE. What baby, then?

KIRSTY. She doesn't have it any more.

EDDIE. Ah, you see. What did she do with it?

KIRSTY. She gave it away.

EDDIE. For adoption?

KIRSTY. Kind of.

EDDIE. When was this?

KIRSTY. When she was at uni, up in Leeds. She was nineteen.

EDDIE. Why? Why didn't she do the decent thing and look after it?

KIRSTY. She tried. She tried really hard. She just couldn't do it, I guess.

EDDIE. What about the father? Where was he?

KIRSTY. Not around.

EDDIE. Didn't your dad do the traditional thing and smash his face in?

KIRSTY. No. They were very supportive, as it happens. But she's never told them who it was.

EDDIE. What, never?

KIRSTY. No. They never knew. They still don't know.

EDDIE. To this day?

KIRSTY. No. We never breathed a word.

EDDIE. We?

KIRSTY. Yes.

EDDIE. So she told you?

KIRSTY. Yes.

EDDIE. Who the father was?

KIRSTY. Yes.

EDDIE. And where is this baby now?

KIRSTY. He's not a baby any more.

EDDIE. Obviously.

He?

KIRSTY. Yes.

EDDIE. So where is he?

KIRSTY. I told you, she gave him up.

EDDIE. Where? To whom?

KIRSTY. What's it to you?

EDDIE. I don't know. What is it to me? Why are you telling me this?

Enter RALPH *and* CAT.

CAT. Couldn't persuade her.

RALPH. Said she had to be up at six bathing the turkey.

CAT. Defrosting it.

EDDIE. I minded your pints.

CAT. So – where were we?

KIRSTY. About to toast your handiwork, Ralph.

EDDIE. And Richard's.

RALPH. And Richard's.

CAT. Cheers!

KIRSTY. Cheers!

ALL. Cheers!

They drink.

EDDIE. What about Tom? Where's he?

CAT. Oh yes – where's Tom? The Keeper of the Wishbox?

EDDIE. Poor Tom.

CAT. Why 'poor Tom'? Oh, you mean, chopping sprouts –

EDDIE. 'Poor Tom that eats the swimming frog, the wall-newt and the water. That in the fury of his heart when the foul fiend rages, eats cowdung for salads and drinks the green mantle of the standing pool.' Where is he?

KIRSTY. I'll go and get him.

It's not far off midnight. He wanted to open the wishbox.

RALPH. Any chance of another? And a double whisky?

KIRSTY. Sure.

EDDIE. And can I have a Guinness while you're at it?

KIRSTY. Cat?

CAT. No thanks, I'm fine.

Exit KIRSTY.

Are you okay?

EDDIE. Yes. Yes, I'm fine.

RALPH. Think I'd better visit the conveniences.

Exit RALPH.

CAT. What were you talking to Kirsty about?

EDDIE. Old times.

CAT. Oh really?

EDDIE. It's okay.

I don't fancy her and she thinks men are shit.

So I'd say you're pretty safe.

CAT. You're in a weird mood.

EDDIE. No I'm not.

CAT. Yes you are.

EDDIE. It's you, not me. You're being weird. I'm not the one being weird.

CAT. Fine. Forget it.

Enter TOM.

Hi. We heard you were still working like a Trojan.

TOM. Christmas dinners.

CAT. You shouldn't be working now. You should tell your boss it's illegal.

TOM. She'd sack me.

CAT. That's not legal either. Would you like a drink?

TOM. Kirsty's getting me a lime and soda.

CAT. You did a great job. It's looking lovely.

TOM. Does your dad like it?

EDDIE. Yes, he does. He really likes it.

CAT. You should talk to him again about that thing you mentioned earlier, about doing carpentry – the recommendation.

EDDIE. What thing?

TOM. I thought if Ralph could tell my mum and dad –

CAT. He's had a drink or two, now might be a good time.

EDDIE. Tell your mum and dad what?

TOM. Tell them – he thought I could do it. That I can make things. Wooden things.

I don't want to do catering.

CAT. Ask him now. Just say it to him again.

Enter RALPH.

RALPH. You did well with your wishbox. Got quite a few customers.

CAT. Did you put one in, Tom?

TOM. No. Not my own.

There is one I'm putting in – for someone else.

CAT. What's that?

TOM. It's upstairs. I'll just go and find it.

Exit TOM.

CAT, EDDIE *and* RALPH *are left at the table*.

EDDIE. Tom wants you to help him, Dad.

RALPH. What's that?

EDDIE. Tom. He wants you to help him do carpentry. Get trained. What do you think?

RALPH. Well, there's no money in it.

EDDIE. No, but do you think he could do it?

RALPH. How would I know? I'd have to see something he'd made.

CAT. I think that's why he brought his box to the house, earlier. For you to have a look at it, see what you thought. So you could perhaps discuss it with his parents or something.

EDDIE. You could do that, couldn't you, Dad?

RALPH. I didn't have a proper chance – I'd have to look at it again.

EDDIE *goes over and gets the wishbox and gives it to him.*

RALPH *examines it again.*

It's nicely turned out.

EDDIE. But what would you say?

RALPH. Got care in it. Attention to detail. Technically sound. Nice feeling to it – the colour, and – proportions . . .

EDDIE. Right then. So you could do that for Tom, then? Tell his parents you'd support his idea?

RALPH. Well, hang on a minute, I'm not promising I can . . .

EDDIE. Oh, come on. Why not? Be a bit of use to someone, why not?

Enter KIRSTY *with more drinks.*

Dad's happy to help Tom.

RALPH. What?

EDDIE. You'll talk to his mum and dad about the carpentry thing. Having seen what he can do.

RALPH. I don't see that it's my place to go against –

EDDIE. Oh, come on, Dad. It's not that complicated.

Why can't you just tell the kid you'll help him?

RALPH. I'm not inciting some young boy to go against his parents' wishes, all right?

EDDIE. What about his wishes?

KIRSTY. It's all right for you to get his hopes up.

EDDIE. It just sounds to me like he deserves a chance.

KIRSTY. Tom can't always – He can't always do the things he thinks of.

EDDIE. But he can provide cheap labour for your bistro?

CAT. Ed.

EDDIE. Why are you playing games with me?

KIRSTY. I'm not playing games.

EDDIE. Yes you are.

KIRSTY. Truth hurts.

EDDIE. So come on then. Let's hear it.

CAT. What's going on, Eddie?

EDDIE. I'm going for a slash.

Exit EDDIE.

KIRSTY. We might have to make this the last one, actually. If that's all right.

RALPH. That's fine, of course. We'll drink up.

KIRSTY *collects the empties and leaves.*

Pause.

RALPH *and* CAT *drink their drinks.*

CAT. So I gather you know Dublin?

RALPH. Oh yes. Spent some happy times there. Derek Marston from my college days, him and me were pals and he was a Cork man. So we used to take our bikes and nip across from Bangor on the boat, weekends or holidays. Spend a bit of time in Dublin and then head out west. Holy Ireland. Land of saints and scholars. Good times.

CAT. You should come over and visit us some time. You and Angela. Come for a long weekend.

RALPH. What about himself? I doubt he'd be glad to see us.

CAT. Of course he would.

RALPH. I'm glad your teaching's going well anyway. A noble calling, if you can stick it out.

CAT. I'm not sure I can, that's the problem.

RALPH. Course you can.

CAT. I had this thing at St Joseph's last summer with one of the kids in my class –

RALPH. I only wish my son could sort himself out.

Get himself a proper career. Stop drifting. Make some decisions.

I don't know what the hell is wrong with him really.

CAT. He is making decisions. Everything he does is a decision.

RALPH. I remember there was this one time with Derek . . . perhaps our second year at Bangor? And we'd gone up to the mountains in Mayo with our tent and we had the little bottle of whisky and were taking slugs of it, and Derek was stirring the soup in the billycan and now and again he'd pour a drop in. So we were looking forward to our supper! And we'd been watching these poor people climbing Croagh Patrick, in their bare feet like they do, with the blood running down, and Derek was ribbing me saying about how soft the English were compared to the Irish and I said Derek you could never do that in your bare feet in a million years and Derek shook me by the hand and said he'd do it before he was fifty and I said ten quid says you're on, and we shook on it. And every year I'd send him a card at Christmas – 'Where's my ten quid?' And every year there'd be a card from him saying – 'Another fourteen years – or whatever – the bet still stands!' – and it was this standing joke. And one year – this was years later – and Derek was in Guildford by then, Head of Maths at the Technical College, good job, you know, he and Valerie had the three girls, all of that, and I sent a card saying – 'Twelve months and counting! Where's my ten quid?' and Derek's card said – 'July's the month. See you in Mayo and bring your tenner! The socks are off and the feet are ready!' And I'd even got as far as finding out about flights to Mayo, and I'd earmarked the weekend in July and was about to tell Angela – And this letter came in the post from Valerie, saying Derek had died, quite suddenly. Heart attack. Getting up to switch off the telly.

So.

And I had this mad thought in my head to go anyway and climb Croagh Patrick. Do it for him or something. In his name or something. I don't know. Just to – To honour – the laughs we had. The time.

CAT. And did you?

RALPH. No. You know the way. Commitments. Busy.

Why do they do it, make their feet bleed?

Who's it for?

CAT. For God, I suppose. Or for themselves.

To show they're sorry.

RALPH. Sorry for what?

CAT. For their sins.

RALPH. And what do they hope to get for it? The blood?

CAT. I suppose – grace.

RALPH. Grace.

What does that mean?

CAT. Mercy.

RALPH. Mercy.

I should climb it then all right. I should rip the bloody things to shreds.

Rip them into shreds and scatter the blood on the railway line.

But what's the use? What's the use?

The dead don't hear. Don't speak. Don't answer back. Deaf to our pleas. Cold-shouldered from the grave. And I can't bring him back.

I saw him go and I did not call him back.

And I think – Did he run through the marsh and curse my name? Did he see me as he died? They say young men, young soldiers, only call for their mothers when they die. They call for God and their mothers. Never the father.

Because I saw him go, you see, I saw him on the night he died. Running out into the night from the workshop. Hopping over the fence at the bottom of our garden and out towards the path to the marsh, the snowy woods. The railway line. We'd had this row. He had some girl or other on his mind and I had . . . They'd got in trouble, she was – up the duff, in trouble, whatever. And this girl needed him, or claimed she did, so we'd had this row about it and I had said don't be such a bloody fool – you've got a place! To do architecture! You've got a chance! These things happen all the time and even if it's true – even if you were the one responsible – there were ways. Of dealing with it. And that's what made him mad. Pelted off howling and I –

I shouted after him. Go, you bloody fool – go, you fool, you want to waste your life then go, I wash my hands. I wash my hands.

He had this orange coat and I saw just one bright flash of it – I saw him running. Out towards the marsh. The railway. The crossing.

And that moment has been visited on me –

I have paid for that moment ten thousand times. Ten thousand times. All the suffering of hell.

How much blood would I have to shed for that? How many times would I have to climb Croagh Patrick for that?

CAT. I don't know. Perhaps – once.

RALPH. Just once?

CAT. Once might do it.

Re-enter EDDIE.

EDDIE. Is it time to go?

CAT. I think so.

Enter KIRSTY.

KIRSTY. You're off now, are you?

RALPH. Yes, we're making tracks, thanks for – Good luck tomorrow. Happy Christmas.

KIRSTY. Happy Christmas! Thanks again.

EDDIE. See you then.

CAT. Thanks a million.

KIRSTY. No problem. Good to see you.

CAT. Bye then.

KIRSTY. Really nice to meet you. Bye. Happy Christmas.

They get their things and leave, as KIRSTY *continues tidying up.*

Enter TOM *carrying a battered rucksack with a CND symbol on it.*

What happened to you?

TOM. I had to get the . . . Where have they gone?

KIRSTY. They had to go home, it's late. They've just gone home.

TOM. Why? They can come back, why can't they come back?

KIRSTY. No, no, it's getting late, Tom. Listen. We all have to go to bed.

TOM. But we haven't –

KIRSTY. I've just got to check the kitchen. Could you do me a favour and just finish in here?

TOM. Finish in here.

KIRSTY. And can you check the locks and switch off the lights when you're done, Tom? Please? Okay? And then it's bedtime. It's been a long day. Time for bed now, okay?

TOM. Okay.

KIRSTY. Thank you.

KIRSTY leaves.

TOM takes the wishbox down from the table and kneels with it beside the crib scene. He opens the rucksack and takes out a folded piece of paper. He opens it and reads it.

Re-enter EDDIE; in the gloom, he doesn't see TOM. Heads to the table to get his hat and scarf.

As he goes to leave he sees TOM.

TOM finishes reading the letter and carefully refolds it.

Then he takes out a bundle of material – something wrapped up in a bright pink scarf.

EDDIE watches him.

KIRSTY enters and sees EDDIE watching TOM.

KIRSTY meets EDDIE's gaze.

EDDIE. Tom. Is that your rucksack?

TOM. Yes.

EDDIE. Can I see?

KIRSTY. Eddie –

EDDIE. Where did he get these?

KIRSTY. Eddie, I'm sorry.

EDDIE. Where did these come from?

KIRSTY. They were Nicola's. I found them. Just recently. They were still in our bedroom.

EDDIE. But it's – These were –

KIRSTY. Things from Richard. It's stuff he gave her.

EDDIE. How has Tom got hold of them?

KIRSTY. I thought he should have them.

EDDIE. So it is Tom.

KIRSTY. Yes.

EDDIE. Nicola's baby. Tom is the baby.

KIRSTY. Yes.

EDDIE. Richard's baby?

KIRSTY. Yes.

EDDIE. Tom. It's me.

TOM. I know you.

EDDIE. Yes. Yes. I know you do. I know you too. Tom. Tom.

Where did you go?

Where have you been?

Where did you go?

TOM. I haven't been anywhere.

TOM *picks up the letter.*

EDDIE. Is that yours too?

TOM. Yes. All of it.

EDDIE. Do you know who it's from?

TOM. It's to Nicola. It says 'love from Richard'.

EDDIE. When? When did he write it?

KIRSTY. The night he died. I was there. I met him out in your garage. Because I'd come over with a message from Nicola – she was in a complete state about being pregnant and she'd decided to get rid of it but she couldn't face telling him herself so she asked me to do it. So I told him. And then he just sat down and wrote the letter and said would I take it back to her. So I did and then the next thing we heard was that he'd – About the accident.

EDDIE. Tom.

The person who wrote that was my brother.

He was my brother and he died.

I'd like to read the letter.

Can I read your letter?

I would really like to read your letter.

TOM. No. It has to go in here. With all the wishes.

He posts the letter into the wishbox.

TOM *smiles and unwraps the bright pink scarf. Out tumbles the carved infant Christ.*

He sets it in the empty manger.

Now.

Blackout.

Scene Four

The sitting room.

Darkness.

Slides of shivering children on wet Welsh beaches – Richard and Eddie, six and ten.

More slides of Eddie and Richard on bikes and trikes; picnics; school play; birthday parties. Seventies polyester shirts. Utterly unremarkable suburbia.

Growing up.

ANGELA *sits in the dark operating the slide projector.*

A slide of Richard, perhaps thirteen, in school uniform.

ANGELA *pauses on that slide.*

Noise of the front door being opened with a key and the other three coming in.

RALPH (*offstage*). . . . an extra two or three hundred cars every day so you can imagine the noise has been – Not to mention the fact that they're slowing at the junction, you see, they slow to turn on Park Road, to make that right turn . . .

Enter CAT *and* EDDIE, *taking their coats off, followed by* RALPH, *in mid-flow, snapping the lights on so that the slides fade.*

ANGELA *switches off the slide projector and wipes her nose.*

ANGELA. Hello, dear.

RALPH. Still up? I'd've thought you'd be in bed by now.

ANGELA. I was just popping up the camp bed and so on for Eddie and Catherine –

RALPH. Where is it then?

ANGELA. What?

RALPH. The bed.

ANGELA. Oh, I – Yes, it just needed a . . . Here we are . . . (*She starts setting up the folding bed.*) So how did the crib look? Did they set it up nicely?

CAT. It was lovely, yes. Wasn't it, Ed?

RALPH. Shame you missed it.

ANGELA. I'm sure I'll get to see it before long . . . they won't take it down straight away, will they? Surely not. Anyway, the hot water's been on, so if you wanted a bath, Catherine, I thought you might fancy one, so I switched on the immersion –

CAT. That would be nice, actually, yes, if you're sure . . .

ANGELA. I thought you might what with that long drive and what-have-you so I've put a yellow towel for you out on the bathroom stool, and that other red one –

RALPH. I'll just go up then and brush my teeth.

Exit RALPH.

ANGELA. Fine, right you are, dear – the red one on the towel rail is for Eddie. Did you hear me, dear? The red one's for Eddie. He won't be long, we tend to have our showers in the morning, so he'll be out in a sec . . . You can hear the light switch go, he won't be a minute –

CAT *helps* ANGELA *set up the bed.*

EDDIE *sits, still in his coat, not helping.*

Now, duvets . . . I brought two down in case one of you decides to take the sofa – I thought you'd better have one each, depending on what you . . . Yes, a shame, but it was just a bit late for me tonight that's all, with everything to be done here – There we go. That's the light switch – Ralph's finished. Must be a record. I'd go on up now if I were you, dear. I'll do these last bits down here.

CAT. Okay. Night, then.

ANGELA. See you in the morning, dear. Sleep well.

CAT. Thanks. And you.

Exit CAT.

ANGELA. I hope you'll be reasonably comfortable anyway. It's not ideal but . . .

ANGELA *finishes making the bed.*

EDDIE, *still in his coat, continues to sit.*

So I'll say goodnight then.

She's a lovely girl.

Catherine.

I'm happy to see you so happy.

I always knew you would find someone. I always hoped.

Is she the one, do you think?

EDDIE. What's 'the one'?

ANGELA. Well, you know. A keeper. One to hang on to. Perhaps – get married. Have children.

Like your dad and me.

EDDIE. Yes I understand. The concept.

ANGELA. We've not done so badly.

EDDIE. No.

ANGELA. Had some lovely years. Some lovely moments.

EDDIE. Yes.

ANGELA. Still switching out the light together. As they say.

What's the matter, darling?

What is it, sweetheart?

EDDIE. Richard.

ANGELA. I know.

EDDIE. I miss my brother.

ANGELA. I know.

EDDIE. Where did he go?

ANGELA. I don't know, my darling.

EDDIE. Why did he go?

Stupid bastard.

ANGELA. No, he wasn't, he wasn't . . .

EDDIE. Why didn't he bloody look?

ANGELA. It wasn't his fault . . . someone made a mistake – They should have done a safety review of that crossing and they didn't, and I'm – I'm on the case, darling, I'm chasing them, I'm fighting them . . .

EDDIE. Fighting who?

ANGELA. The Council.

EDDIE. Why?

ANGELA. Because it's somebody's fault and somebody out there knows it.

EDDIE. That is so English!

ANGELA. What?

EDDIE. 'I blame the Council'!

ANGELA. Well, I do.

EDDIE. The Council didn't kill Richard.

ANGELA. Somebody did.

EDDIE. I don't think so.

ANGELA. People don't just die like that!

EDDIE. Yes they do.

ANGELA. What – completely out of the blue! For no reason?

EDDIE. Yes. People die for no reason all the time. All the time. It's as common as rain. He just didn't look.

Or else –

ANGELA. Else what?

EDDIE. Or else he looked.

ANGELA. And what?

EDDIE. Chose.

ANGELA. Chose what?

EDDIE. Chose to go.

ANGELA. Don't say that.

EDDIE. Why not?

ANGELA. It was 'death by misadventure'. That's all anyone has ever said.

EDDIE. 'Misadventure.'

ANGELA. Yes. And I know that someone is to blame. Not Richard. Not your father. Not me. Someone out there.

EDDIE. Someone out where?

ANGELA. Someone who should have made sure that the proper safety measures were – that the safety review of the crossing they said was to take place in 1986, took place. And it didn't. The decision which the Railway Safety Committee put their names to in August 1985 re. the marsh path level crossing over the railway line – and I know this because I've seen the minutes of that meeting, I insisted I saw the minutes – that decision was not actioned. Somebody failed to take action. And Richard lost his life. And somebody must pay. On their knees. I want someone to look me in the eyes and say I am responsible and I am sorry. I am sorry that your heart has been broken and broken and broken. I want someone to say the words.

EDDIE. There's no one to say it, Mum.

ANGELA. There is.

EDDIE. There isn't.

There's you and me and Dad.

And whatever secrets Richard had –

ANGELA. He had no secrets.

EDDIE. Something happened tonight.

ANGELA. Where? What?

EDDIE. Something happened to me. In the pub.

ANGELA. The pub?

What happened?

EDDIE. I saw something. I understood.

ANGELA. What?

EDDIE. Tom.

ANGELA. Tom?

EDDIE. Tom Ellis. At The Greyhound.

ANGELA. What has he got to do with anything?

EDDIE. Nicola had a baby. Did you know that? She had a baby at university.

ANGELA. Did she really?

EDDIE. Up at Leeds. In her first year.

ANGELA. What's that got to do with us?

EDDIE. Tom is that baby.

ANGELA. What – Kirsty's brother? The boy who was here earlier?

EDDIE. Yes, but he's not her brother.

ANGELA. He obviously must have been a very late addition to that family. A mistake, perhaps, I suppose Kirsty's mum must have been in her forties –

EDDIE. Nicola had the baby but she couldn't look after him, so their mum took him. And let people think he was hers. A late addition. Unexpected. Premature, whatever.

ANGELA. That sounds highly unlikely.

EDDIE. Mum.

ANGELA. It's not uncommon. You get a bit careless when you're that age, you assume you can't get pregnant, at forty-plus, you just think, well I'm past all that, so she probably took a risk, Mrs Ellis, or a half-conscious – decision – or whatever –

EDDIE. Tom is Nicola's son.

Nicola and Richard's.

ANGELA. I mean, who knows, you don't want to condemn someone for going ahead, for bringing a life –

EDDIE. Nicola was pregnant. Richard got Nicola pregnant. Tom is their son.

ANGELA. Even though – forty-plus, I mean it's not the optimum age, not when you know about the risks and so on but –

EDDIE. Tom is Richard's son.

Richard left a son.

Tom is what is left to us of Richard.

ANGELA. No.

EDDIE. Isn't that a good thing?

ANGELA. No. Not Tom. No.

EDDIE. Why not?

ANGELA. Because . . .

My child is gone.

MY child.

Do you understand?

EDDIE. So that makes Tom your grandchild.

ANGELA. No.

EDDIE. Isn't it what you wanted? A grandchild. Something of Richard.

ANGELA. Not like this. Not this mess.

EDDIE. Mess?

ANGELA. And Nicola . . . Nicola . . . The cause of all the trouble in the first place.

EDDIE. So, here we get to it.

ANGELA. He had a place to do architecture! He could have been an architect!

I'm not surprised she got herself pregnant, first year at university –

EDDIE. 'Got herself pregnant'?

ANGELA. She was fast.

EDDIE. Fast.

ANGELA. Cheap. You saw those outfits she wore. The shoes and the bird's-nest hair and the – bedroom eyes.

EDDIE. It was the eighties. She was a teenager, she was a girl, she wore eyeliner . . .

ANGELA. She was after him.

EDDIE. Or he was after her.

ANGELA. She could have had an abortion.

EDDIE. But she didn't. She had a baby.

ANGELA. Having sex behind my back.

EDDIE. Where did you want them to do it – in front of you?

ANGELA. They shouldn't have been doing it at all.

EDDIE. Teenagers have sex. That's what they do.

ANGELA. Well they shouldn't. We didn't.

EDDIE. Course you bloody did. Or you would have if you could have.

ANGELA. He was always so good before. Drawing and making things. Such a good little boy. My good son.

EDDIE. Jesus.

ANGELA. And I don't believe a word of this anyway. This insane – allegation – about that poor little handicapped boy.

EDDIE. 'Poor Tom.' Chopping up sprouts in Kirsty's fucking kitchen. And Dad won't even help him out of there.

ANGELA. It's not true.

EDDIE. The truth is messy.

Mess is essential to truth.

ANGELA. Don't lecture me.

This has nothing to do with me.

EDDIE. We have something left. We have something left of him.

ANGELA. I'll show you my file from the Council.

EDDIE. I don't want to see it.

ANGELA. I'll prove it to you.

EDDIE. I don't want proof. I'm not touching it.

ANGELA. What I'm doing is real, it's about justice, it's about the truth for Richard.

EDDIE. He doesn't care! Richard's dead! What's it to him? Letters to the Council! This is real. This is flesh and blood.

ANGELA. I don't want any more of this dangerous lie about that boy at the pub.

EDDIE. You say you want the truth for Richard. Well here it is, right here in front of you, living and breathing. Here is the truth.

ANGELA. I can't. I won't believe this.

EDDIE. What were you doing all night anyway? Instead of being there for Dad? Or putting up the guest bed for Cat and me? What were you doing? Moping all night?

ANGELA. I was doing nothing.

EDDIE switches on the slide projector and bangs off the light switch.

EDDIE. Was it this? Was this the nothing you were doing?

ANGELA. Don't touch that!

EDDIE. There's no one there, Mother! Those people are gone.

ANGELA. That's not yours and this is not your house.

EDDIE. It's a trick of the light. The people in the pictures have all gone. It's just the wall. It's the wall, for Christ's sake!

ANGELA. Don't you swear at me!

EDDIE. You've spent the night staring at the fucking wall!

EDDIE hits the light switch and the image on the slide fades out.

See! Gone! Nothing there! Nothing! Get rid of this crap. It's time it was gone.

EDDIE unplugs the slide projector and sweeps it up, carrying it out of the back kitchen door.

Enter RALPH in pyjamas and dressing gown.

RALPH. What's going on?

ANGELA. Nothing . . . nothing, dear.

RALPH. What's he on about now?

ANGELA. Let's just leave it.

RALPH. It's Christmas Eve, for Christ's sake.

ANGELA. Ralph –

RALPH. Who does he think he is, behaving like this in my house on Christmas Eve?

Enter CAT, in pyjamas and cardigan, with wet towel.

CAT. Is everything all right?

ANGELA. Eddie's a bit upset. He said something happened at the pub.

CAT. Really?

ANGELA. Do you know what happened, dear?

RALPH. I thought he was unnaturally quiet in the car on the way home.

ANGELA. Perhaps it's coming back home. Richard and the twenty years and Christmas and everything. Anniversaries. They always stir things up again.

CAT. Where's he gone?

ANGELA. I don't know. At least he's got his coat on.

CAT. Perhaps I'd better go and see if –

ANGELA. Don't you go out, dear, not if you've just had a hot bath. You'll get pneumonia. Go and see if he's all right, dear, will you?

RALPH. What, now?

ANGELA. Yes, go on, go and see if he's all right. He might be in the garage, he was taking that slide thing out.

RALPH. We should just let him cool off.

ANGELA. I don't want him doing anything silly. Please, dear. Go and talk to him. Will you please? I don't want him to hurt himself. Go and see if he's all right. Please.

RALPH *goes to leave.*

Don't go without your –

ANGELA *runs off to hallway.*

RALPH *and* CAT *wait for her to come back, frozen with embarrassment.*

ANGELA *comes back with his coat.*

RALPH. Thanks.

He puts the coat on and leaves.

ANGELA *sits.*

ANGELA. None of this ever goes away. Ever.

I knew it was a mistake to get those carvings out.

I knew she was up to something.

CAT. Who was up to something?

ANGELA. That girl, the Ellis girl from the pub. Kirsty. And now the boy, the one in the kitchen, Tom. Why come knocking at the door asking for them now? Why, now?

I knew she was after something. They were always after something, those girls.

The pair of them, hanging round my boys.

And now look what's come of it.

CAT. What has come of it?

Ring at the doorbell.

ANGELA. Would you go and see who that is, dear?

CAT *goes to get the door.*

She comes back in with KIRSTY.

KIRSTY. I'm sorry. I know it's very late.

I can't find Tom. He ran off. I wondered if he'd come here.

ANGELA. Here? Why would he come here?

KIRSTY. Because . . .

ANGELA. I don't know what you said to my son tonight, but Eddie's in a terrible state and one thing I can tell you is that I do not need this, not on Christmas Eve, not the first Christmas that Eddie has come back to see us in God knows how long –

KIRSTY. I know, I'm sorry, it was a mistake. I didn't mean it to happen tonight it just – It all got out of control.

ANGELA. What? What is out of control? What have you said to him?

KIRSTY. I didn't say anything. He saw; he just knew.

ANGELA. Saw what? What did Eddie see?

KIRSTY. My sister's stuff.

KIRSTY *takes out the CND rucksack and takes from it the pink scarf and the carved Baby Jesus.*

ANGELA. Oh, God.

KIRSTY. It was all still there in our bedroom, all the things Richard had given her, she must have hidden them away, not touched them again. I found all this stuff at the back of the cupboard.

So I gave them to Tom, I thought he should have them. But I didn't mean for all of this to come out, I didn't mean to – hurt you.

ANGELA. Oh, didn't you?

KIRSTY. It's just – being back home. And all the letters and pictures and secrets, and Nicola's still a mess, she's still, she's on the phone to me saying not a day goes by, after all this time not a day goes by she doesn't think of him.

CAT. Of who – of – ?

KIRSTY. Of Richard. After twenty years. And Tom. He was her baby. He was their baby. And he gets treated like this – idiot and I'm to blame, too. I'm part of it, too.

So once Eddie knew, I just thought, Tom has to know, I have to tell him. So I did.

CAT. Just now? Tonight?

KIRSTY. I told him everything and I said I was sorry and I went to get him a drink and when I came back he was gone and I don't know where he is but I thought – perhaps he's come back here, to talk to Eddie or something, he might have cut along the back way through the marsh – and over the crossing – But if he'd done that he ought to be here by now.

CAT. Eddie's out in the garage, perhaps we should –

ANGELA. If he came by the marsh path, he'd have come over the fence at the bottom of the garden. He might have gone straight to the garage.

KIRSTY. Could I go and see if –

A cry of pain and commotion at the back door.

RALPH *stumbles in.*

His hands are bleeding quite profusely.

ANGELA. Ralph, what's happened? What have you done?

RALPH. It's all right – it's all right – I need a towel or –

CAT. Here –

RALPH. It's going on the carpet –

ANGELA. Don't be stupid, that doesn't matter – What have you done? What's happened? Have you – Did somebody – Is there somebody out there? What happened?

RALPH. Yes – it was – It's all right – I was packing away the crates in the garage –

ANGELA. My God, Ralph, what have you done – what have you done – ?

KIRSTY. Is Tom out there?

RALPH. Tom? Yes, yes, he's out in the garage, him and Eddie –

KIRSTY. Is he all right?

RALPH. He's fine.

KIRSTY. Tom's all right? Are you sure?

RALPH. He's with Eddie, he's fine.

KIRSTY. Let me have a look. Just let me look.

ANGELA. What were you doing out there?

RALPH. Taking out the nails. From the tea chests. The knife slipped and –

KIRSTY. What kind of knife?

ANGELA. What did I tell you about those? What did I tell you?

RALPH. Aaah –

KIRSTY. It's all right, it's all right, I've seen worse. It's okay. But we need to bind him up – do a tourniquet – and keep your hands up, Ralph, just keep them up really high, like that, that's good – and then Angela – we need some –

RALPH. It's all going on the carpet – I'm sorry –

ANGELA. Oh, shut up, Ralph, it doesn't matter –

KIRSTY. We need some – something to wrap – Do you have bandages – or – can you cut up a pillowcase or something? Anything – just something clean?

ANGELA. Oh yes, yes –

Exit ANGELA.

RALPH. This is a lovely visit you're having.

CAT. Never a dull moment.

RALPH. We aim to please.

KIRSTY. How are you doing, Angela?

ANGELA (*offstage*). I'm not sure if I've got the right –

KIRSTY. Perhaps I'd better . . . Can you keep your hands up?

CAT. Shall I – ?

KIRSTY. Yes. Just help him keep them right up high, that's good.

Back in a minute.

Exit KIRSTY.

RALPH. Got my blood now.

CAT. Sorry?

RALPH. Not exactly Croagh Patrick.

CAT. I see.

RALPH. Hurts though.

CAT. Yes, I'm sure.

RALPH. I saw him coming in. Like a film going backwards. Tom.

He came back in – over the garden fence.

Bright flash of his coat coming back towards me. Back over the fence. Up the garden path. Into the workshop. Back towards to me. Coming up the path towards me. His face!

He was holding the –

Like everything in reverse, like rewinding the tape . . .

(*In pain.*) Ah.

CAT. But what happened?

RALPH. The knife slipped.

CAT. But how did you – ?

RALPH. They were helping me.

And the knife slipped. And there was a nail – The nails –

CAT. Do you want some water?

RALPH. No. This is good.

This is good.

No water.

Mercy.

Grace.

Enter KIRSTY *and* ANGELA, *tearing up pillowcase into strips, etc.*

KIRSTY *starts to make tourniquet.*

ANGELA. He looks a bit pale. Ralph? Ralph – are you – ?

KIRSTY. Get him some water.

ANGELA. Oh, darling, oh, my darling –

KIRSTY. He's okay, it's all under control. Get this bound up and we'll be fine –

CAT. Should I just go out and make sure the boys are all right?

ANGELA. Boys?

CAT. Eddie and Tom. They're in the garage.

ANGELA. Oh yes, dear. Yes. Good idea.

Take your coat, dear.

CAT puts her coat on and leaves.

ANGELA *makes a cold compress and gets a glass of water and goes over to* RALPH.

RALPH. That feels all right.

ANGELA. Good.

Poor old wounded soldier.

RALPH. Bloody fool.

KIRSTY. Okay, this is the hard bit.

Salty water. We're going to clean this out.

ANGELA. Brace yourself, Ralph.

KIRSTY. Now.

Starts cleaning out the wounds as RALPH *grimaces.*

Sorry.

RALPH. No, it's all right. That's good.

KIRSTY. Don't want to leave anything nasty in there.

RALPH. No indeed.

ANGELA. You're very good at this.

KIRSTY. I work in kitchens. Lots of knives.

RALPH. Making food for hungry mouths.

KIRSTY. It's a living.

RALPH. It's a good thing.

Making food for people.

We live, we die. Get a few nice meals in between. What else is there?

KIRSTY. I suppose.

RALPH. I'm grateful to you.

KIRSTY. That's okay.

RALPH. No, I mean. We are grateful. For what you've done.

KIRSTY. I didn't mean –

RALPH. Doesn't matter what you meant. You did what needed to be done. That's the thing.

KIRSTY. You need to keep those up high for a few more minutes. Help it to stop.

RALPH *holds his hands up high.*

RALPH. My arms are getting tired.

ANGELA *helps him by supporting one elbow.*

KIRSTY *supports the other elbow.*

ANGELA. Thank you, dear.

Blackout.

Scene Five

The workshop, as it was left at the end of Scene One – tidied by
RALPH, *but the three empty tea chests are still there.*

EDDIE *staggers in with the slide projector, bangs on the light.*

Puts the slide projector down in the middle of the floor. Sits next to it on the floor, defeated.

Then he plugs it in and starts clicking the carousel forward through the slides.

Gets to empty space and the blank square of light is thrown against the wall.

EDDIE *stares at the empty space.*

Then he clicks on.

We get back to the first slide of Richard – as in Scene One – cigarette, laughing. EDDIE *clicks forward. Pictures of Nicola and Richard – the party, the pink scarf. First Nicola, then Richard wearing the pink scarf.*

Enter RALPH – *unwounded – wearing coat over his pyjamas and dressing gown.*

RALPH. So. You obviously got what you came for.

Congratulations.

EDDIE. For what?

RALPH. Your foot hardly in the door twenty-four hours and you've managed to upset your mother twice with your ructions.

Why do you have to do it?

Why do you have to goad everybody all the time?

Why do you have to make us suffer?

We're happy to see you. We want to see you. We wanted you to come. We've waited years for you to be here at Christmas.

EDDIE. You never seem very happy to see me.

RALPH. We are. Of course we are.

EDDIE. You seem to hate everything about me.

RALPH. We want you to be happy.

EDDIE. I am . . .

I could be.

RALPH. If what?

EDDIE. I don't know.

RALPH. Your mother has suffered. More than you can know.

EDDIE. Then why won't she – listen.

RALPH. Listen to what?

EDDIE. To what I'm telling her.

RALPH. You mean this thing in the pub tonight?

EDDIE. Yes.

RALPH. You saw something? You heard something? Somebody said something?

EDDIE. Yes.

RALPH. What then?

EDDIE. I think you know what. I think you both know.

RALPH. Know what?

EDDIE. I think you've always known. Both of you.

RALPH. What?

EDDIE. You're going to make me spell it out?

RALPH. Spell it out, go on.

EDDIE. Richard's son. He left a son.

RALPH. What son?

EDDIE. Tom. Tom Ellis, at The Greyhound.

It's Tom.

Isn't it?

RALPH. You tell me. You seem to have all the answers.

EDDIE. What was he thinking? Why didn't he just say that his girl-friend was pregnant? Christ, it happens all the time, it's no big deal, not enough to do this to us. Stupid, stupid bastard. Stupid – child. Why didn't he look where he was going? If it was a mistake. And if it wasn't –

RALPH. No, Eddie, no –

EDDIE. If, I'm saying, if – if he chose – if he chose to walk out in front of a train, why didn't he – tell us? So we at least could know the fucking score. So Mum needn't waste twenty years badgering the Council about safety reviews and – making a file that thick of wasted time, wasted fucking phone bills, wasted anger, wasted days and days and days –

RALPH. Son.

EDDIE. But tonight when I looked at Tom it was like . . . there he was.

I used to think about Richard every day, picture his face every day, so I'd remember what he looked like, but then it got harder and harder so in the end I stopped.

And then when I was nineteen, I thought – that's it. He never made it this far. I've overtaken him; I'm older than he ever was. We've swapped. My older brother is my younger brother. Younger and younger every year.

You think it doesn't hurt me, you think it doesn't hurt, to see you cling and cling and fucking give up on everything else, on life, on me. And I hate him for it, I hate him, I fucking hate him for it. Ruining our lives. Switching out the light so we live in this dark all the time.

RALPH. Don't hate your brother. He did try to tell me.

He said there was some girl and they'd got in trouble. And I said tell her to get rid of it. There's no need to feel guilty. You could be an architect! Everything we've done for you – shelling out on – the French exchange and the skiing trip and the extra maths – Who did that for me, eh? Who did that for me?

I made him so mad and he runs off and that's the last . . . And I'm stood here shouting . . .

So you see – it's me. It's me that is cursed.

And if he took his own life – if that's what he did – it's me who must pay.

And I'm paying – every day.

Do you see now?

I'm the one to be angry with. Not your brother. Not your mum. Me.

EDDIE. Why don't you tell her?

RALPH. It would destroy her.

EDDIE. She wants someone on their knees saying sorry. That's what she says she wants.

RALPH. But if she thought it was my fault that –

EDDIE. Your fault that what?

RALPH. That he . . .

EDDIE. That he died? That you drove him to it?

RALPH. Yes.

EDDIE. That he confided in you and you betrayed him?

RALPH. Yes.

EDDIE. That if it hadn't been for what you said he'd be alive today?

RALPH. Yes.

Do you think that's the truth?

EDDIE. It might be.

RALPH. It's out now.

EDDIE. Say it to Mum.

RALPH. I can't.

EDDIE. It might stop her bugging the Council.

RALPH. It would kill her. It would kill me. I can't.

EDDIE. Perhaps it was just an accident. Perhaps he just didn't look. 'Misadventure.'

RALPH. Yes, perhaps.

EDDIE. Do you think that?

RALPH. I try to think that.

Some days I do think that. Almost.

EDDIE. Me too.

So you knew about Nicola. You knew what was going on.

RALPH. He talked about some girl who was pregnant, I don't know if names were mentioned.

I suppose I did know. I suppose I knew there was something going on with him and that girl Nicola. But – she'd gone away by then, she was in Leeds –

EDDIE. But did you never want to talk to her afterwards? Find out what happened?

RALPH. Our boy had died, I wasn't – thinking.

EDDIE. You didn't want to find out?

RALPH. I think I thought – Maybe I thought – she must have – dealt with it. Made her choice. It somehow didn't seem my business. (*He starts.*) What's that?

EDDIE. Is it a fox?

RALPH. No. There's someone out there.

Someone's coming.

Give me that torch.

Someone just jumped the fence.

Jesus.

EDDIE. Who is it?

RALPH. Christ . . .

Enter TOM. *He is carrying the wishbox.*

EDDIE. Tom. You gave us a fright.

TOM. I came the back way. I came through the marsh.

EDDIE. How could you even see to put one foot in front of the other?

TOM. I know the way.

EDDIE. It's not very safe. You shouldn't go that way at night. It's not safe.

TOM (*offering wishbox to* EDDIE). It's nearly midnight, we can open it.

Don't you want to?

EDDIE. Yes I do want to.

How do we – ? Is it locked? Is there a key?

TOM *takes out a screwdriver and starts unscrewing the box.*

Should we really read out people's private letters?

TOM. They want them read.

EDDIE. How do you know?

TOM. They wrote them because they need them to be heard.

EDDIE. Tom . . . perhaps we shouldn't read out all of them.

RALPH. Did you put one in yourself, Ed?

EDDIE. No. Cat did.

RALPH. I suppose they're meant to be anonymous.

EDDIE. Dad –

TOM. There. Go on. You first.

EDDIE *puts his hand in and pulls out a card.*

RALPH. What's it say?

EDDIE. 'A bissicle a red one fank you Maisy.'

TOM. A bicycle.

EDDIE. Now what?

TOM *pulls out a cigarette lighter and lights the corner.*

RALPH. Hey, you can't do that in here – Get rid of that – you'll have the house burnt down –

RALPH *grabs a tin bucket and holds it underneath the burning piece of paper.*

TOM *drops the burning paper into the bucket. With a brick he bangs out the flame.*

TOM. All done. Your go.

RALPH *puts in his hand and pulls out a card.*

RALPH. 'Dear whoever's reading this – my wish is for world peace, obviously, and second, please can we not have a row on Christmas Day?'

TOM *burns it and uses the brick to stamp out the flame.*

TOM. Now. You.

EDDIE *puts his hand into the box and takes out the letter in the envelope.*

RALPH. That one must be a mistake, it looks like a proper letter.

EDDIE. Dad, it's Tom's, it's –

RALPH. Do you want it read out?

TOM. Yes.

RALPH. Right you are then. Go on then, Eddie.

TOM. Go on.

RALPH. What's the matter?

TOM. Read it.

EDDIE. I – can't – I can't – I don't want to –

RALPH. What's the matter?

EDDIE. You do it.

RALPH. Come on, Eddie, we'll be here all night.

EDDIE *opens the envelope, takes out the letter and looks at it.*

EDDIE. 'December 22nd. Dear Nicola. It's nearly midnight and I wish you were here. I wish – '

RALPH. Full of wishes, anyway.

EDDIE. 'I wish I could say to you all the things that your letter made me – '

RALPH *takes the letter from* EDDIE.

RALPH. December 22nd.

EDDIE. Dad.

RALPH. Whose is this?

TOM. Mine.

RALPH. Where d'you get this from?

TOM. Kirsty. She found it in her bedroom, back of the cupboard with the Baby Jesus. She gave them to me, said I could keep them.

RALPH. Oh did she?

RALPH *holds the letter. Then gives it back to* EDDIE.

Let's hear it.

EDDIE. We don't have to.

RALPH. We do.

EDDIE. 'Dear Nicola. It's nearly midnight and I wish you were here. I wish I could talk to you. I wish I could say to you all the things that your letter made me feel. Nick, you don't have to do this. You think you have to but you don't. Sometimes I am in despair when – '

RALPH *covers his face with his hands.*

RALPH. Oh God, no, no –

EDDIE. ' – when I think of all the things our child will never see or smell or touch or do; when I think of all the things he could have been in his life and all the sunsets he'll never see and all the jokes he'll never hear, it makes me wish I could die in his place – '

RALPH *grabs the letter from* EDDIE *and the cigarette lighter from* TOM *and starts to burn the letter.*

TOM. No!

TOM *grabs for the letter;* RALPH *holds it away from him.* TOM *grabs* RALPH'*s wrist and forces it down, trying to take the letter off him. They struggle.*

RALPH. Eddie . . . Eddie – help me . . .

EDDIE, *frozen, watches helplessly.*

TOM *forces* RALPH'*s hand down onto the top edge of one of the tea chests where there's a large nail still sticking up.*

RALPH *bellows in agony as the nail goes into his hand.*

TOM *picks up the burning letter and drops it into the bucket, then pounds it with a brick to put out the flames.*

Jesus Christ!

RALPH *can't move – he is pinned to the tea chest.*

TOM *has succeeded in putting out the flames. He picks up the remains of the letter from the bucket. There are only a few charred remains – unreadable.*

Eddie, help me.

This hurts, Eddie, please . . .

With an effort, RALPH *pulls his hand off the nail.*

TOM *cradles the remains of the letter.*

TOM. No, no, no, no, you shouldn't have done that.

RALPH. I'm sorry. I'm sorry.

TOM. I am in despair, I am in despair –

RALPH. I'm sorry, Tom, it's just, I can't hear it. I can't.

TOM. 'I am in despair when I think of all the things our child will never see or smell or touch or do; when I think of all the things he could have been in his life and all the sunsets he'll never see and all the jokes he'll never hear, it makes me wish I could die – '

RALPH. I thought you couldn't –

EDDIE. Ssssh.

TOM. ' – die in his place if it would do any good but I know it
wouldn't. I can only say please, please, Nicola, think again and
don't do this. Wait for me to get there so we can talk. As soon as I
can get away I'm coming over – wait for me. My dad says be an
architect, be an architect, but I don't want to, I want you, I want, I
wish, I wish this could be – a beginning and not an end.

A beginning and not an end.

All love

Always

Richard.'

Then RALPH *walks to the tea chest. Pushes his other unhurt hand
down onto the nail.*

EDDIE. What are you doing?

RALPH. It's all right. It's all right.

He pulls his hand away from the nail. Nurses his two wounded hands.

EDDIE. It was an accident, Dad. He didn't mean to. It was an accident.
Wasn't it?

RALPH. Yes. It was an accident.

You made a nice job of that wishbox.

TOM. I've made other things. Hundreds of things.

RALPH. What sort of things?

TOM. Toys. Animals. Birds.

RALPH. Where are they?

TOM. At home in the shed.

RALPH. You show me some time.

TOM. I will.

RALPH. You show me and I'll see what I can do.

TOM. Talk to my parents?

RALPH. Yes.

TOM. About what we said earlier.

RALPH. Yes, all right.

TOM. Tell them what you think.

RALPH. I will.

TOM. And a reference?

RALPH. If that's what you need.

TOM. Please.

RALPH. I will. You're a good boy.

I'm all right. Don't worry, Edgar. There's a good boy.

Both of you – good boys.

Exit RALPH.

EDDIE. What about the rest?

TOM. We should read them.

EDDIE *picks one out*.

EDDIE. 'A new washing machine. Thanks!'

TOM *burns it*.

'My Christmas wish is for Daddy to come home for Christmas. Yours sincerely, Andrew.'

TOM *burns it*.

'My Christmas wish is to pass my driving test, cheers, hope someone's reading this.'

TOM *burns it*.

'Mum well again, all I want for Christmas.'

TOM *burns it. As he does so,* CAT *enters and stands in the doorway, watching*.

CAT. Your dad's inside, bleeding all over the carpet.

EDDIE. Is he all right?

CAT. I think so. What happened? What are you doing?

EDDIE. Emptying the wishbox.

CAT. You're not reading them?

EDDIE. We are.

TOM. We read and then we burn.

CAT. Aren't they people's secrets?

TOM. People write them because they want them to be heard.

CAT. Can I see one?

EDDIE shows her the one in his hand. CAT reads it. EDDIE picks up the hammer.

EDDIE. Perhaps we should bang these down. They seem to be a health hazard.

CAT. Where I come from we'd have called these prayers.

She gives it back to TOM, *who burns it.*

EDDIE. Prayers are for the faithful. On this island we have wishes.

CAT. What about mine? Did you read mine?

EDDIE. Something about a washing machine?

CAT. That was it.

EDDIE. I don't need to read yours. I know what yours is.

They leave.

TOM *picks up the wishbox and empties it.*

There is one last remaining card.

TOM. 'And the prophet said: Your children are not your children. You are the bows from which they as living arrows are sent forth. You may house their bodies but not their souls. For their souls dwell in the house of tomorrow. Do you hear me, Eddie? Don't be afraid.'

TOM *picks up the lighter. Burns* CAT*'s card. Drops it in the bucket and watches it burn.*

The slide of Richard and Nicola is still on the wall.

It's the last thing we see as the lights fade.

The End.

A Nick Hern Book

The Six-Days World first published in Great Britain in 2007 as a paperback original by Nick Hern Books Limited, 14 Larden Road, London W3 7ST

The Six-Days World copyright © 2007 Elizabeth Kuti

Cover design: Ned Hoste, 2H

Words quoted by Eddie on page 52 taken from *King Lear* by William Shakespeare

Words quoted in Cat's letter on page 87 taken from *The Prophet* by Kahlil Gibran

Typeset by Nick Hern Books, London
Printed and bound in Great Britain by Biddles, King's Lynn

A CIP catalogue record for this book is available from the British Library

ISBN 978 1 85459 557 7